Julia Wolf
The Paradox of False Belief Understanding

Epistemic Studies

Philosophy of Science, Cognition and Mind

Edited by
Michael Esfeld, Stephan Hartmann, Albert Newen

Volume 50

Julia Wolf

The Paradox of False Belief Understanding

The Role of Cognitive and Situational Factors for the
Development of Social Cognition

DE GRUYTER

ISBN 978-3-11-128008-0
e-ISBN (PDF) 978-3-11-075861-0
e-ISBN (EPUB) 978-3-11-075865-8
ISSN 2512-5168

Library of Congress Control Number: 2021943077

Bibliographic information published by the Deutsche Nationalbibliothek
The Deutsche Nationalbibliothek lists this publication in the Deutsche Nationalbibliografie;
detailed bibliographic data are available on the Internet at http://dnb.dnb.de.

© 2023 Walter de Gruyter GmbH, Berlin/Boston
This volume is text- and page-identical with the hardback published in 2022.
Printing and binding: CPI books GmbH, Leck

www.degruyter.com

Acknowledgements

I have had the great fortune of having the support of a wide number of people for this work, which was initially submitted as my doctoral thesis at the Ruhr University Bochum. Firstly, I owe great thanks to my supervisors Albert Newen and Stephen Butterfill. My primary supervisor, Albert Newen, has supported and guided me from the beginning of this project. His passion for research serves as a constant source of inspiration. The advice and critical comments from my second supervisor, Stephen Butterfill, have been invaluable in substantially improving my work. I am very fortunate to have been able to benefit from feedback from two such prominent experts in the field during my doctoral studies.

Before coming to Bochum, I was lucky enough to have some excellent philosophy teachers who inspired me to continue studying philosophy. I thank Lizzie Fricker and Ralph Walker for encouraging me to continue in philosophy and Anita Avramides, who started off my interest in the problem of other minds, thereby setting the foundation of this research.

Many thanks also to Alan Leslie and his lab at Rutgers University, who I visited in my second year of studies. I learned a lot in the discussions at the lab meetings. Alan Leslie was also the one to suggest looking at pretend play, so he had a significant influence in shaping Chapter 6. At this point I must also thank the Research School at the Ruhr University Bochum who funded my research stay at Rutgers University.

I was fortunate to be able to complete my studies in the context of the DFG Funded Research Training Group 'Situated Cognition' (GRK-2185/1), which came with the benefit of a ready-made support network of PhDs and Post-Docs. I thank all of them for the comments and discussion at the various RTG workshops. Special thanks go to Beate Krickel for all her work in keeping the RTG running and her advice on life as a PhD student, as well as Elmarie Venter and Matej Kohar for their useful comments on the manuscript and making sure to get me out of the house occasionally while writing the thesis. You are the best office mates I could have asked for.

Thank you also to everyone at the *Lehrstuhl* for Philosophy of Mind at the Ruhr University Bochum for the many hours of discussion. A special thank you goes to Sabrina Coninx who went above and beyond in reading and commenting on large parts of this thesis. In the course of writing a joint paper with Albert Newen, we have had much discussion about the role of mindreading, which I also benefited from in writing this thesis. I also thank Tetiana Adler, Valerie Zarges, and especially Yasmin Schwetz for all their kind help and patience with administrative matters.

https://doi.org/10.1515/9783110758610-001

Throughout my doctoral studies, I have had the opportunity to present my work at a number of workshops and conferences, and benefited from attending the vast number of workshops taking place at the Ruhr University Bochum. I thank the audiences for their feedback and comments.

In the later stages of my studies, I was able to join the D-A-CH project 'The Structure and Development of Understanding Actions and Reasons' (NE 576/ 14 – 1). In the context of this, I also benefited from the many interesting paper discussions in the "*Lesekreis*", as well as their comments on the Situational Mental File Account. I especially thank Josef Perner, Michael Huemer and Martin Doherty for the many discussions of the false belief task and mental files at workshops over the years.

Finally, I owe a very big thanks to my parents, who supported me uncondi- tionally throughout my journey. Not only have they provided a constant source of motivational support, they have also always been willing to read and discuss my work. There would be many more typos and grammatical errors in this work without their help in proofreading this thesis. I would never have reached this point without them. Thank you!

For my parents

Contents

List of Figures and Tables

https://doi.org/10.1515/9783110758610-002

List of Acronyms

FBT	False Belief Task
IT	Interaction Theory
ST	Simulation Theory
ToM	Theory of Mind
TT	Theory Theory

https://doi.org/10.1515/9783110758610-003

Introduction

Humans are social creatures. We live in groups and are constantly interacting with other people. As such, social cognition – our ability to understand and interact with others – is a fundamental part of our everyday life. What makes this topic especially interesting is that the way in which we understand or interact with other people seems different to the way in which we think about and interact with objects. For example, we understand others not just as moving objects, which obey certain physical rules, but also as *people* with mental states, which guide their actions. So, for example, when I see my friend going to the fridge, I do not interpret this merely in terms of some physical laws and regularities (although these may be an underlying cause), but in terms of his desire for a snack. Similarly, I think of myself in terms of mental states too. For example, when I get up and go to the living room, I interpret this in terms of my *desire* to get my book and the *belief* that my book is in the living room.

The questions of *how* we achieve such an understanding of others, *what* this involves and *when* it develops are questions, which have long since exercised philosophers and psychologists, leading to some highly fruitful interdisciplinary research. Central to this has been work in developmental psychology looking at the development of social cognition in children. The reason for this is that looking at how children develop an understanding of others, might in turn tell us something about what this activity actually consists in. For example, one of the big questions prompting my research on this topic was the philosophical question of how it is even possible to come to an understanding of other people in terms of mental states (see Avramides, 2001, for discussion of this problem). Looking at how this understanding actually develops in children, what influences this development and where things go wrong might help in answering at least some parts of this question.

The development of social cognition is a vast research area. My focus here will be on a specific but important component of this: namely the development of children's ability to attribute beliefs to others and understand their behaviour in terms of these beliefs. This is considered an important part of our everyday social cognition and often referred to as *mindreading* or *Theory of Mind* (ToM) in the literature.[1] The development of mindreading is most commonly studied by testing children's ability to attribute false beliefs to others in the context of the false belief task (FBT). I will go into more detail concerning this task and

---

1 I will predominantly make use of the term 'mindreading' rather than 'Theory of Mind' in this work.

https://doi.org/10.1515/9783110758610-004

why research on the development of social cognition is important in Chapter 1. For now, however, I will only briefly introduce the main ideas of the task. The FBT tests children's understanding of beliefs by testing whether they are able to attribute a false belief to someone else and predict their behaviour based on this. This means that in order to pass the FBT, the child must be able to attribute a belief to the other person, which diverges from reality and understand that the other person's behaviour is determined by that belief and not reality. For example, in the classic version of the FBT (see for example Baron-Cohen, Leslie, and Frith, 1985; H. Wimmer and Perner, 1983), children watch a puppet place their toy in one location. The puppet then leaves and while she is gone, the toy is moved to another location or removed from the scene entirely. The puppet returns and the child is asked where the puppet will search for her toy. The key finding from these studies was that children before the age of 4 systematically fail these kinds of tasks, leading to the widespread view that children's understanding of belief develops at age 4 (Wellman et al., 2001).

In recent years, however, this interpretation has been called into question by new 'implicit' versions of the FBT. Contrary to the classic 'explicit' versions of the FBT, which directly ask children to predict someone's belief, or to predict their behaviour based on this belief, implicit FBTs are usually indirect and non-verbal tests of children's belief understanding. Infants at 15 months and younger have been shown to master some of these tasks (Onishi and Baillargeon, 2005; Scott, 2017). This leads to the so-called 'paradox of false belief understanding', which has led to an ongoing debate in the literature concerning the development of children's belief understanding:

> These findings give rise to a very interesting and widely debated 'developmental paradox': if young infants already understand false belief, as the [implicit] spontaneous-response FBT suggests, then why do they fail the [explicit] elicited-response FBT? (de Bruin and Newen, 2014, 298)[2]

In other words, if the implicit FBT provides evidence of belief understanding – as it has sometimes been claimed to do – why do children still consistently fail a very similar task pertaining to test the same ability. It should be noted that calling this the paradox of false belief understanding does have to mean that this is something specific to *false* belief understanding as opposed to belief understanding in general. The reason why I refer to the paradox of false belief under-

---

2 De Bruin and Newen (2014) refer to the implicit FBT as "spontaneous-response FBT" and the explicit FBT as "elicited-response FBT". In Section 2.3, I discuss why I think this terminology is problematic and therefore opt for talking in terms of implicit-explicit FBTs instead.

standing is that belief understanding in this context is tested by the ability to attribute false beliefs.

My central aim in this book is to develop the Situational Mental File Account to provide an explanation of this developmental paradox and in doing so provide an outline of the development of children's belief understanding up to age four.

1 The Paradox of False Belief Understanding

When considering this paradox, one question which has been and continues to be hotly debated within the literature, is the nature of the development underlying the paradox of false belief understanding. Is it a development of belief understanding, with children either gaining a first understanding of belief or reaching a new level of belief understanding? Or is it something else that develops? Does the implicit FBT really show belief understanding or not?

I will be addressing these issues in Chapters 2–4. It should be noted, however, that my focus will be on belief understanding as the *ability* to attribute beliefs to others and, which *processes* underlie this. This might differ somewhat to some of the literature where there is often a focus on the question when children acquire a *concept* of belief (Apperly, 2011). There are a number of reasons for this. Firstly, the criteria for determining whether someone has a concept of belief are unclear (Apperly, 2011). For some time, passing the explicit FBT was considered the criterion for having a concept of belief, but with the early success of infants in implicit FBTs this cannot be taken for granted. If we want to look at whether the child has a concept of belief, the problem is not only whether we have the adequate evidence for this, but that it is not even clear what evidence we would need.

Secondly, as Samson and Apperly (2010, 446) state, for social cognition "being able to use one's ToM is as fundamental in reasoning about mental states as having ToM". This can be seen in some studies with adults where, under certain circumstances, adults have been shown to perform poorly on tasks requiring belief attribution even though they clearly have the concepts in question (see Samson and Apperly, 2010, for discussion). In order to engage in everyday social cognition, it is not sufficient to merely have a concept of belief. I must be able to use it, and doing so will incur all kinds of demands going beyond mere concept possession. These "demands are inherently part of the processes required to reason about other people's mental states" (Samson and Apperly, 2010, 446). Similarly, young infants have been shown to pass implicit versions of the FBT and it is at least an open question whether they have a concept of belief at this point.

Therefore, having a concept of belief may be neither necessary nor sufficient for the performance we see in the FBT.

Thirdly, the question I am interested in is *how* belief understanding develops and which processes underlie it. Apperly (2011) notes that answering the question when the concept of belief develops does not necessarily tell us very much about the processes which underlie this. My approach here will therefore be to develop an account in terms of the processes, which underlie the paradox of false belief understanding. Only later, in Chapter 4, will I return to the question of whether this development should be classed as a development of belief understanding and at which point children should be credited with an understanding of belief.

2 The Role of Cognitive and Situational Factors

What are the processes underlying the paradox of false belief understanding? Broadly, we can find two different factors, which underlie this development and which are widely discussed in the literature. On the one hand, there is internal cognitive development (cognitive factor), which plays a role in the development of belief understanding. On the other hand, the situational context (situational factor) also affects the development of belief understanding.

I will be arguing for the Situational Mental File Account as an empirically adequate account of the paradox of false belief understanding. This account builds on the recent work of Perner et al. (2015, Perner and Leahy, 2016) who make use of the mental files framework – which I will introduce in more detail in Chapter 4 – as a means of thinking about cognitive development also in the context of the explicit FBT. I make use of this framework as it allows for a more detailed investigation of the cognitive re-organisation underlying the development of belief understanding. I modify and extend their account to consider the role of situational factors within this development. I will argue that this active consideration of both cognitive and situational factors and how they interrelate in development is something that is crucial for explaining the paradox of false belief understanding but has thus far been neglected in the literature.

At this point, it is worth noting that the role of the situational context for cognition has been the subject of increased interest, especially within the school of "Situated Cognition". As I will not be arguing for a specific form of Situated Cognition, I only mention this debate here briefly. The views under the umbrella of Situated Cognition come in different shapes and strengths. Broadly speaking, these Situated Cognition approaches take the view that we cannot understand cognition as that of an isolated individual (the most extreme example being the brain in a vat), but that we must consider the wider bodily (embodied cognition) or environmental context (embedded and extended cognition) as well as the dynamic interaction of the person with her environment (enactive cognition). One of the contentious issues between different views is the question whether the environment has a causal role or a constitutive role in cognition. For example, embedded cognition is the view that in order to understand cognition, we not only need to consider the individual, but the interactions of the individual with his physical and social environment (Rupert, 2009). This may, however, merely be a causal influence that the environment exerts. A more extreme view is that of extended cognition, which asserts that – at least some parts of – the environmental context are a constitutive part of cognition (Clark and Chalmers, 1998). This shifts the boundary of the mind and cognition to beyond the brain and body to include also the situational context. While I share the view that consideration of the environment is an important part of understanding cognition, I want to remain neutral on whether this forms a constitutive part of cognition or merely exerts a causal influence.

As a theoretical background for my project, I will therefore take a Scaffolding View (Sterelny, 2010), which places a considerable emphasis on the role of the environmental context, but is neutral concerning the causation/constitution issue. On this view, cognition is actively influenced by the environment. Importantly, this is not only a passive process by which our environmental context influences cognition, but also an active one where we shape and change our environment, generating 'ecological niches' so as to provide optimal conditions. For example, when setting out to work on this book I can make my environment as distraction free as possible, so as to not have to deplete cognitive resources in order to maintain focus. The upshot of this is that a systematic change in performance need not be due to an internal cognitive development, but also due to a systematic restructuring of the environment. For the purposes of this discussion, a central idea is that not only are our thoughts shaped by the environment, but we also shape our environment and can thereby, indirectly, shape our thoughts. This will be a guiding principle especially when considering how cognitive development occurs and how it interacts with situational factors.

It should also be noted, however, that some of the situated cognition approaches are critical of the view that belief attribution is a central part of social cognition and have argued that the FBT may not measure an important form of social cognition. Especially on enactive and embodied views of cognition, we do not require mindreading for social cognition. Mental states are embodied and can therefore be directly perceived, with social cognition taking place in the interaction between agents without requiring any attribution of mental states (Gallagher, 2001; Hutto, 2004). Furthermore, it is alleged that the FBT is an artificial task that goes wrong in trying to exclude precisely the situational influences our normal cognition depends on. I will discuss these views and their criticism of mindreading in Chapter 1, where I will defend the role of mindreading and the FBT especially as an important element of research into the development of social cognition. Furthermore, I argue that situational factors also play a key role within the FBT, which we need to adequately consider in order to provide an account of the paradox of belief understanding.

I will now provide a brief outline of the book, the heart of which lies in establishing the Situational Mental File Account (Chapter 4 onwards).

3 Outline

In Chapter 1, I discuss the relevance of the paradox of false belief understanding. I defend mindreading as a core strategy of social cognition, and the FBT as a valuable measure of this. While mindreading is not our only means of understanding others, it nonetheless has an important and distinct role in our understanding of others, warranting special research.

In Chapter 2, I then move on to examining the paradox of false belief understanding itself and the empirical literature that gives rise to it. I review the different types of FBT and highlight some of the similarities and differences between FBTs. While most of the literature considers only two different types of FBT (implicit and explicit), I identify *three* different categories of FBT, which differ in the demands they pose, with active helping behaviour FBT paradigms providing evidence of an intermediate stage between implicit looking behaviour based FBTs and explicit FBTs. The differences in performance on these tasks suggests that there are three stages that can be highlighted in a continuous development of belief understanding. I also consider some of the objections often made against the implicit FBT, in particular concerns about their replicability.

In Chapter 3, I consider previous accounts of the paradox of false belief understanding, focusing on the role of situational and cognitive factors within these accounts. While individual accounts do consider cognitive and situational factors, these have not been integrated sufficiently. As such, accounts of the cognitive development or the situational factors underlying the change in performance are largely independent. Instead, I argue that cognitive and situational factors must be considered in conjunction when providing an account of the paradox of false belief understanding.

Having clarified the paradox of belief understanding and highlighted some of the problems with previous accounts, I propose the Situational Mental File Account in Chapter 4, which forms the central part of this book. This account makes use of the mental files framework as a means of providing a more detailed account of the cognitive development underlying the paradox of false belief understanding. Perner et al. (2015, see also Perner and Leahy, 2016) have already fruitfully applied this framework to the FBT. I extend their discussion in two important ways. Firstly, I consider the role of situational factors within this framework, both directly on children's performance as well as on the cognitive development itself. I argue that situational factors play an important role in the cognitive reorganisation of mental files – which underlies the paradox of false belief understanding. Secondly, I argue for an intermediate stage of belief understanding in terms of a uni-directional linking in order to account for the intermediate stage of the active helping behaviour paradigms.

Extending this discussion, in Chapter 5 I elaborate on the mental files framework. Using literature from perspective taking, I consider how the ability to represent the mental states of others develops and how this relates to our representations of our own mental states. Specifically, I argue that we are able to represent another's perspective by creating a vicarious mental file early in development. The ability to relate this perspective to our own (implemented through a linking of mental files) is a later development.

Finally, in Chapter 6, I broaden the discussion to consider pretend play. This has been suggested to pose similar demands to belief understanding (Leslie, 1987) and may therefore provide a useful ecologically valid paradigm to validate the findings from the FBT. I highlight some of the similarities and difference between belief attribution and pretend play and argue that children's early pretend play can be fruitfully characterised in terms of uni-directional linking between mental files, thereby providing further support for the intermediate stage put forward in Chapter 4.

1 The Significance of the False Belief Task

The main aim of this book is to develop an empirically adequate account of the *paradox of false belief understanding.* This paradox refers to the finding that children fail explicit versions of the false belief task (FBT) till age 4, but pass implicit versions of the same task much earlier. The aim in this chapter is to set the groundwork for the discussion of the paradox of false belief understanding from Chapter 2 onwards by showing that the paradigm giving rise to the paradox remains an important tool for testing the development of social cognition. In other words, in this first chapter, I will be concerned with the question *why* we should be interested in the findings from the FBT, thereby providing a background motivation for the discussion of the paradox of false belief understanding to follow in the next chapters.

The FBT has held a central position in the literature on the development of social cognition for more than 30 years. It has become the staple test of whether children have an understanding of the mental states of others or not. In recent years, however, there has been mounting criticism against the FBT, arguing that the FBT is an overly artificial measure that is unable to tell us anything about how social cognition really works and develops. In this chapter, I will argue that although there are reasons to be apprehensive of the dominance of the FBT in the study of the development of social cognition in children, the FBT remains a relevant and useful task that continues to give rise to interesting new insights concerning the development of cognition.

In this chapter, I will first review some of the history of the FBT and clarify what exactly the FBT is supposed to test. This will give me the opportunity to introduce some of the central terms in this debate: *mindreading* and *social cognition,* and how these relate to each other. Based on this, I will then address some of the criticisms against the FBT, the main criticism being that the FBT is an inadequate test of social cognition that does not reflect the realities of everyday social cognition. Concerning this I will argue for the importance of mindreading, and that the FBT, as a measure of mindreading, does test an important aspect of social cognition. Having thus defended that FBT paradigm, I will then turn to focus on the paradox of false belief understanding from Chapter 2 onwards.

1.1 Social Cognition, Mindreading and the False Belief Task

Broadly understood, social cognition refers to our ability to understand other people. It is the basis of our ability to interact with others – both in a cooperative

https://doi.org/10.1515/9783110758610-005

and a competitive manner, and our ability to predict and explain the behaviour of others. Traditionally, it was thought that social cognition is fundamentally based on mindreading, i.e. the ability to attribute mental states such as thoughts, beliefs, desires, or emotions to others. It is only in recent years that the idea that social cognition might not be based solely on mindreading has gained in popularity. The debate surrounding mindreading can be traced back to the seminal Premack and Woodruff (1978) paper, "Does the Chimpanzee have a Theory of Mind?" Premack and Woodruff were interested in the question whether animals (in this case, chimpanzees) were able to attribute mental states to others and make use of this to predict the behaviour of others. They famously coined the term 'Theory of Mind' (ToM) for this ability of an individual to "imput[e] mental states to himself and others" (Premack and Woodruff, 1978, 515). In the literature, Theory of Mind is used interchangeably with the terms 'mindreading' or 'mentalizing'. I will predominantly use 'mindreading' to refer to this ability to attribute mental states to oneself and others,[1] in keeping with my focus on mindreading as an ability rather than a matter of concept posses- sion (see Introduction).

It is critical to note that the term 'mindreading' has two meanings in the de- bate. Understood widely, mindreading refers to the ability to attribute any mental states to another person, including mental states such as thoughts, desires, emo- tions, and beliefs. This is the way I defined it above. Understood narrowly, mind- reading refers to the ability to attribute beliefs to another person. The attribution of beliefs (narrow mindreading) is a subtype of the attribution of mental states (wide mindreading). Someone who is not able to attribute beliefs might still view others as minded beings and be able to attribute mental states other than beliefs. Someone who lacks the ability of mindreading is not able to attribute beliefs. For the sake of clarity, I will reserve the term 'mindreading' for mindreading widely understood unless otherwise specified. When talking about mindreading narrow- ly understood, I will refer specifically to belief attribution.

What is the role of the FBT? In order to understand the significance of the FBT it is important to understand how and why it came about. In the previously mentioned paper, Premack and Woodruff (1978) carried out an experiment to test whether chimpanzees were able to infer the intention of another individual and predict their behaviour accordingly. Their specific methodology is not important for our current purposes. What matters is that in response to this study the FBT

---

1 Although mindreading refers to the ability to attribute mental states to oneself and others, my focus in this book will almost exclusively be on attributing mental states to others, leaving open whether and how we attribute mental states to ourselves.

was independently suggested by Dennett (1978), Bennett (1978), and Harman (1978) as a means of avoiding some of the criticisms that had been raised against Premack and Woodruff's experiment, and thereby provide conclusive evidence of the ability to attribute mental states to others. The crucial element of the FBT is that it exploits the fact that beliefs can be false. Therefore, it allows for introducing a distinction between the other's belief and reality (or one's own knowledge of reality). Therefore, for example, the chimpanzee sees Bob place his banana in the crate, but the banana is then removed without Bob's knowledge so that Bob believes the banana is in the crate – which the chimpanzee knows to be false. If the chimpanzee is predicting behaviour on the basis of beliefs, the chimpanzee should expect Bob to go looking for his banana in the crate (even though the banana is not actually in the crate).

It should be noted that in exploiting this distinction between belief and reality, the FBT was intended to provide a particularly stringent test of mindreading by means of testing belief attribution. Failure to pass the FBT is insufficient to show that someone is able to engage in mindreading widely construed.[2] If a child fails the FBT they might nonetheless be able to attribute other mental states such as desires to another person and therefore be capable of at least some forms of mindreading widely construed, even if they cannot engage in mindreading narrowly construed (i.e. belief attribution). Moreover, failing the FBT alone is also insufficient to show that someone is incapable of belief attribution (i.e. mindreading narrowly construed). The FBT is a demanding task and there might be a range of reasons why someone capable of mindreading could fail. So, while passing the FBT provides evidence of both wide and narrow mindreading (in virtue of belief attribution being a subtype of mindreading), failing the FBT is not sufficient to show an inability to mindread understood either widely or narrowly.

While initially Dennett (1978) made clear that the FBT was to be understood as a sufficient test of mindreading and not a necessary one, the prevalent view that resulted from the finding that children before the age of 4 fail (at least explicit versions) of the FBT is that children are actually incapable of attributing

---

[2] The exception to this being cases where the FBT has been used with people with disorders such as autism, where there is assumed to be a deficit in mindreading broadly construed. However, in these cases there was usually a previously observed deficit of social cognition in general which is then explained in terms of a deficit in mindreading and tested via the FBT (Baron-Cohen et al., 1985). The view that there is a general deficit in mindreading in these disorders was not based solely on findings from the FBT but also on the previous knowledge of a general social deficit.

beliefs to others prior to this point (Wellman et al., 2001).[3] This view that failing the FBT provided evidence of being incapable of attributing beliefs is something that developed in the literature following a range of variations and modifications of the task (Perner, 1991). This seemed to show that this age 4 boundary was a robust result, persisting across variations. It was this robust finding, which led to the view that there is a genuine change in children's ability to attribute beliefs to others at age 4.

As noted above, the FBT is specifically concerned with mindreading narrowly construed. That is to say, it aims to test the ability to attribute beliefs to others. Mindreading, broadly construed, concerns a wide range of mental states beyond beliefs. Although the FBT may also require an understanding of some other mental states (especially desires), the focus is very much on attributing beliefs as the necessary ability for passing the FBT. While this exclusive focus on beliefs has been subject to criticism (see, for example, Apperly, 2011), it is worth noting that there are at least two reasons for this fixation on beliefs. Firstly, as noted above, by making use of beliefs it was possible to make use of a distinction between beliefs and reality, making the FBT such a powerful test of mindreading broadly construed. The idea was that if someone passed the FBT we could be sure that they were attributing mental states to someone. Tests making use of other mental states, such as in the original experiment by Premack and Woodruff (1978) would not provide as conclusive evidence as the FBT and might be explainable in non-mentalistic terms.[4] Secondly, beliefs are often thought to be particularly important mental states, which are crucial for predicting and explaining the behaviour of others (Doherty, 2008). This is inspired by the influential view of belief-desire pairs as both the cause and explanation of action. While the origins of this view can be traced back to the ideas of Hume (1978), in current discussions this idea is most famously associated with the work of Davidson (1963) and his highly influential arguments that belief and desire pairs (so called pro-attitudes) cause our behaviour. Therefore, for example, it is the desire for a cold glass of water, paired with my belief that there is cold water in the fridge that causes me to go to the fridge to get some water. It should be noted that the question of how actions are actually caused and how we predict and explain the actions of others are at best loosely related. If our actions are indeed caused

---

3 This view became much more controversial following the findings from the implicit FBT, as we shall see in Chapters 2 and 3.

4 Authors such as Povinelli have argued that the non-mentalistic explanations are also possible for the FBT (Penn and Povinelli, 2007; Povinelli and Vonk, 2003). Although he targets implicit FBT paradigms in these criticisms, the same can also be said against the classic explicit paradigms. See Section 1.2.1 for further discussion of this criticism.

by beliefs and desires, then this could provide reason to think that a social cognition based on the attribution of beliefs and desires to others could be effective, but not necessarily so. Similarly, even if actions are not caused by belief-desire pairs we might still make sense of others by attributing beliefs to them. As my aim is to look at the development of understanding of others' actions, not the actual cause of actions, I will not discuss the belief-desire framework further here. Although this framework has substantially fed the discussion surrounding the FBT, the rationale of the FBT does not depend on it and I will neither defend nor assume this framework for the purpose of this discussion.

The basic idea behind the FBT can be summarised as follows: the phenomenon we are ultimately interested in is *social cognition*, which refers broadly to our ability to understand and interact with other people. This ability is thought to be fundamentally based on *mindreading*, i.e. the ability to attribute mental states to others. Belief attribution is a critical subcomponent of mindreading. The best way to test mindreading is through the FBT, which tests mindreading via testing belief attribution. Motivating the FBT, we therefore have the following picture (Figure 1.1):

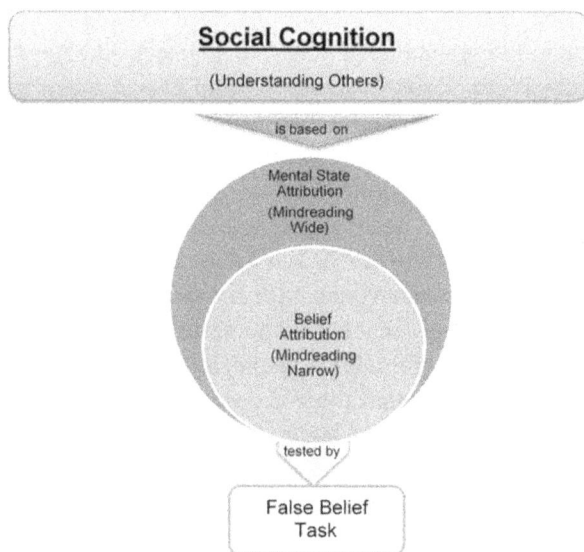

Social Cognition

(Understanding Others)

is based on

Mental State
Attribution

(Mindreading
Wide)

Belief
Attribution

(Mindreading
Narrow)

tested by

False Belief
Task

Figure 1.1: The relation of social cognition, mindreading and the FBT. Social cognition is based on (or occurs via) mindreading. Belief attribution is a sub-type of mindreading. The FBT is the central test of mindreading in virtue of being a stringent test of belief attribution.

It was in light of this, with the FBT as the 'acid test' of mindreading that the FBT rose to prominence and has remained the staple test of mindreading in the developmental literature, in particular following the initial and robust findings of the shift in performance at age 4 (Baron-Cohen et al., 1985; Wimmer and Perner, 1983): not only was the FBT a neat means of testing social cognition, but it also seemed to be picking up an important developmental step.

It should be noted that this simplified picture can be seen as the target of many of the critics of mindreading and the FBT. This is not to say that this view is actually held by adherents of the mindreading account. These views are usually more nuanced and do not claim that mindreading narrowly understood is the sole basis of our social cognition (Apperly, 2011). Rather the claim is that belief attribution is a particularly central social ability (e.g. Doherty, 2008) or that it represents a significant organisational change to the structure of our social reasoning, for example a change to an understanding of *representational* mental states (Wellman et al., 2001).

1.2 Criticisms of the False Belief Task

Based on the above picture, there are two places where one might object to the FBT (see Figure 1.2). Firstly, it might be objected that the FBT is a poor test of mindreading, either widely or narrowly construed. Secondly, it can be objected that social cognition is not actually based on mindreading. Insofar as the FBT does test mindreading, then it does not test any interesting or important aspect of social cognition.

It would be possible to simply accept both of these criticisms and maintain that the research on the FBT paradigm is nonetheless justified. We have a clear and modifiable paradigm that generates a rich literature. The developmental shift we find in the performance on the explicit FBT does appear to be picking out something, even if this is not the central development in social cognition.[5] The FBT generates patterns of data, in particular in the context of the paradox of false belief understanding, which we do not have an adequate explanation of so far. It could be that, rather than picking out something specific about the development of social cognition, the FBT picks out a domain general cogni-

---

5 Some of the critics of the FBT acknowledge this. For example, Hutto (2009, 227) writes, "Without doubt something important happens in normal child development somewhere between the ages of 3 to 5, when false-belief understanding is acquired ... It would be foolish to deny this, but it would be still more foolish to jump to the conclusion that the relevant change (when it occurs) necessarily indicates the pinnacle achievement of ToM mastery".

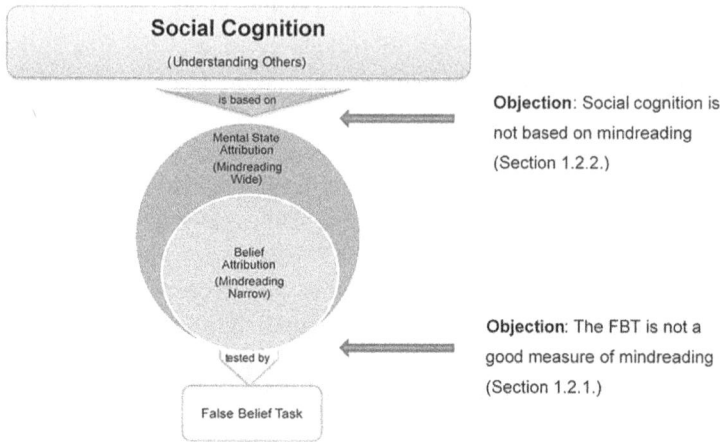

Figure 1.2: Objections to the relevance of the FBT as a test of social cognition.

tive development.[6] In other words, the FBT might be testing the development of an ability that is not specific to the development of mindreading or our ability to understand others, but rather something more general, which underlies belief attribution as well as other abilities that are not related to mental state attribution. On this understanding, the FBT might be thought of as similar to the Dimensional Change Card Sorting Task (Zelazo, 2006), which tests children's ability to switch between rules for sorting cards. In this task, we are not interested in the ability to sort cards according to changing rules per se, but rather in what this tells us about domain general executive function abilities. The same might be true of the FBT in that, even if we are not interested in belief attribution per se, we might still be interested in what this tells us about domain general cognitive developments.

In the remainder of this chapter, however, I want to go further in defending the FBT as a test of social cognition. My main focus will be on the latter criticism that mindreading does not form an important part of social cognition and detailing how this pertains to the FBT. This criticism is often put forward by defenders of the so-called interactionist account (De Jaegher et al., 2010; Gallagher, 2001; Gallagher and Hutto, 2008; Hutto, 2004) but is also echoed in some of the pluralist accounts (Andrews, 2012, 2017; Fiebich, 2015, Fiebich and Coltheart, 2015;

---

6 In Chapter 5, I consider the notion of perspective taking and how this might be an ability underlying performance on the FBT that does extend beyond attribution of mental states and understanding others. See also Perner et al. (2002) for more on this.

Fiebich et al., 2017). However, I will briefly address the former criticism concerning the FBT as a test of mindreading in the next section and highlight some of the issues I will return to in the next chapter.

1.2.1 The False Belief Task as a Test of Mindreading

A number of criticisms can be made against the FBT as a test of mindreading. A first obvious criticism is the focus on beliefs as opposed to other mental states. Naturally, there are problems with making assertions about mindreading widely understood based only on the FBT that only tests belief attribution (i.e. mindreading narrowly understood). I do not deny that tests of the attribution of other mental states are undoubtedly important if we want to gain a complete understanding of mindreading. The FBT alone cannot provide this. That being said, as noted above, there are some good reasons why the FBT is of particular importance, not least, because it is one of the most stringent tests of (wide) mindreading we have.

It is also worth noting that few of the advocates of the FBT would think that the FBT alone could allow us to form a full picture of the development of mindreading. Many acknowledge other mental states, and that children may well be able to attribute other mental states to people before they are able to attribute beliefs (Gopnik and Wellman, 1992; Wellman et al., 2001). This is true especially for desires, which, as we saw above, form the second main component of a belief-desire psychology. It is undoubtedly true that there has been considerably less research on the attribution of other mental states such as desires (but see Repacholi and Gopnik (1997) and Ruffman et al. (2018) for some work specifically on this issue). Here too there are unresolved questions worthy of research. Nonetheless, it remains that belief attribution is an important step in the development of social cognition, which continues to pose puzzles and deserves research.

A second, more fine-grained criticism is that a single-minded focus on the FBT as a means of testing belief attribution is problematic. In other words, this is a call for methodological pluralism in testing belief attribution. One specific version of this criticism is that the FBT is too demanding, which is often found by adherents of a nativist account of belief attribution. This is the view that children may be competent mindreaders but still fail the FBT because of the additional demands of the task (Helming et al., 2016). I will return to this issue when discussing the nativist accounts in more detail in Section 3.3. For now, it should be remembered that one of the initial aims of the FBT was to provide conclusive evidence of mindreading, and therefore err on the side of caution. Furthermore, this objection is less of a concern for us as it does not take the form of a principled rejection of the paradigm per se, but rather calls for modifications. Nativists such as Baillargeon, Carruthers or Leslie do not in general oppose the FBT, rather they suggest potential aspects, which could be modified in order to test whether children are able to pass less demanding versions of the task (Baillargeon et al., 2010; Carruthers, 2013; Leslie, 1994). It is also worth bearing in mind that in the more than 30 years since the first FBT there have been many variations both of the explicit and the implicit FBT paradigms. These will be discussed in Chapter 2 where I provide an overview of the literature from the FBT.

Both of these criticisms call for a more varied approach to testing mindreading – both in terms of testing the ability to attribute mental states other than beliefs and devising alternative means of testing belief attribution. While these criticisms may be valid, they do not threaten the goal of this book, as they do not deny that the FBT is an important component of testing mindreading.

Some criticisms, however, go further than this. For example, Reddy and Morris (2004) have put forward a more principled criticism of the FBT as a means of testing mindreading. They argue that while the FBT was useful as a test when it was initially developed, the excitement about the FBT has caused us to lose sight of the real phenomenon as it takes place in the everyday. They argue that in many more naturalistic settings we can see that infants do have an understanding of the mental states of others, even including beliefs (see also Reddy, 2008, for a review). Children's abilities in these more naturalistic settings should not be ignored just because children fail the FBT, which is an arbitrary and artificial task. Instead, Reddy and Morris stress evidence from early deception, which, they argue, shows that young infants already understand not only some mental states of others but their beliefs specifically.[7]

The problem highlighted by Reddy and Morris is not specific to the FBT, but alludes to a general issue in experimental research. On the one hand, we need to have highly controlled, rigorous studies of a phenomenon to provide valid and replicable results. These, however, are then often artificial and therefore pose problems for the children. On the other hand, we need naturalistic studies of the phenomenon we are interested in. These, however, are harder to control. Such studies are often observational and it may not be possible to modify key variables. Therefore, the interpretation of these findings is more difficult. Ulti-

---

7 I do not want to take a position on the status of early deception here. It should be noted, however, that it is an open question whether this early deception requires a full-blown understanding of belief or whether it should rather be seen as a precursor of belief understanding (see e.g. Perner (1991) for a critical view).

mately, we need both kinds of evidence: both of the tightly controlled lab setting, and from a more ecologically valid point of view. Ideally, the findings should dovetail; in reality, the situation is usually more complex. In the final chapter of this book, I consider pretence and how this relates to belief attribution as measured by the FBT. While by no means considering the full scope of mindreading, going beyond the FBT allows us to develop a more rounded picture of development.

A final criticism I mention here is the criticism that the FBT does not actually provide any evidence of mindreading as children could work out what the other person will do by relying purely on behaviour rules. Povinelli and Vonk (2003) make this principled criticism primarily against non-verbal measures of cognitive abilities in animals pertain to show mental state attribution, for example the tests whether animals can represent the conspecific not seeing an object while oneself can see the object and act accordingly (e.g. Hare et al., 2001). Povinelli and Vonk argue that animals are not representing the visual perspective of conspecifics but are simply sensitive for basic behavioural cues (like where the subject is looking) to explain their abilities. The same criticism also applies to the implicit FBT as used with infants, and even the explicit FBT. After all, the child could also explicitly be predicting what the other person will do based on behaviour rules or what they have seen people do in the past. A first point to note about this criticism is that it too leaves the paradox of false belief understanding untouched: even if Povinelli and Vonk were right in their critique, the difference between performance on the implicit and the explicit FBT would still require explanation.[8] Secondly, this critique depends on setting a criterion for when it is reasonable to attribute a concept of belief to someone (Buckner, 2014). This has led to considerable disagreement in the literature especially on animal cognition, with some authors (such as Tomasello et al., 2003) having less stringent criteria for belief attribution than Povinelli whose criteria are very strict and are not met by any of the current tests of mindreading. Where should one draw the line? It is not my aim to draw a clear line here between behaviour reading and mindreading, so I will only comment on this issue briefly.

---

[8] The same is also true of Tyler Burge's recent critique of tests of mindreading (Burge, 2018). In this paper, Burge argues that the FBT is incapable of providing evidence of belief attribution. It may show that children are able to decouple from their own perspective when anticipating another's action, but this is not sufficient to show that they are genuinely attributing mental states. This is a very strong claim which has received some critical response (Carruthers, 2020; Jacob, 2020). As this criticism applies to both the implicit and the explicit FBT – and indeed to many other experiments pertaining to show that young children have a mentalistic understanding of others – it leaves the diverging findings from the implicit and explicit FBTs unexplained.

One should be careful about setting the standard too high, however, otherwise all social cognition becomes explainable in terms of behaviour reading and belief attribution is superfluous for social cognition, which seems to be incompatible with the important role of belief attributions in everyday life, which these authors do not deny. This would also dissolve the problem at hand because if all social cognition is explainable in terms of behaviour reading, it is unproblematic that the FBT is only a test of behaviour reading. Equally, however, one should be cautious of having too low standards such that everything counts as belief attribution and thus mindreading. An example of what might be a good middle way is suggested by Newen and Starzak (2020), where belief attribution presupposed at least some minimal flexibility and updating ability of the organism.

1.2.2 The Unimportance of Mindreading?

I will now turn to the second criticism, namely that social cognition is not in fact based on mindreading. This criticism originates largely within the interactionist camp, who argue for more direct forms of social understanding, which do not require mindreading. However, there are also attempts to downplay the role of mindreading within social cognition in pluralist accounts. In the remainder of this Chapter 1 will respond to these criticisms and argue that mindreading does play an important role in social cognition.

The Interactionist Criticism of Mindreading

To understand the criticisms of mindreading, it is important to be clear on what exactly is meant with mindreading. As we saw above, mindreading is defined as the ability to attribute mental states (and especially beliefs) to others. It also carries with it the claim that the mental states of others are – to some extent at least – hidden and not directly accessible. The idea is that while we can directly perceive the behaviour of another person, the mental states underlying this are not directly accessible and can only be inferred based on the behaviour. This assumption is shared by two of the main accounts of mindreading, Theory Theory (TT) and Simulation Theory (ST); although they disagree, on how exactly we bridge this gap. In other words, they agree that social cognition depends on mindreading, but disagree about the strategy, by which mindreading is carried out. According to TT, mental states are part of a theoretical framework, which we use to predict and explain the behaviour of others consisting of generalised rules. There are many different versions of TT, ranging from accounts arguing that this theorising takes place within an innate module (see for example Baron-Cohen, 1995; Leslie, 1987) to those who argue that children learn these theories through a process of theory revision in the course of their experience (see Gopnik and Wellman, 1992, 2012). Simulation accounts reject the idea that mindreading is based on generalised theories and instead argue that mindreading is based on simulation, which might be broadly understood as "putting oneself in the other's shoes". We do not need theories to make sense of others as we can use ourselves as a 'model'. Here too there are different accounts, which differ on the role that introspection plays for simulation. For example, Goldman (2006) conceives of simulation as an 'offline' running of our own systems. In order to determine what someone else will think or do. I run my own systems to work out what I would think or do in that situation. I introspect what it is that I would think or do in that situation and then attribute this to the other person whereas introspection is thought to be a direct means of access to my own mental states. Gordon (1986) proposes an alternative simulation account, which does not depend on introspection. I still imagine myself to be in the situation of the other person, but determining what I would think or do does not require introspection. For example, in order to determine whether I think that it is sunny outside I do not need to introspect my beliefs about the weather, but simply answer the question: is it sunny outside? In the current literature, most advocates of mindreading adhere to a hybrid of both TT and ST, where both strategies are used as a basis for mindreading.

Crucially for our current purposes, both TT and ST agree that we only have indirect access to the mental states of others, which we gain via mindreading (implemented as either theorising or simulating). Proponents of interaction theory (IT) object to this (Gallagher, 2001; Gallagher and Hutto, 2008; Hutto, 2004, 2009). They argue that our understanding of others is not indirect, but that we very often can directly perceive the mental states of others. Our understanding of others is "primarily neither theoretical nor based on an internal simulation, but is a form of embodied practice" (Gallagher, 2001, 81).

> In most intersubjective situations, that is, in situations of social interaction, we have a direct perceptual understanding of another person's intentions because their intentions are explicitly expressed in their embodied actions and their expressive behaviors. This understanding does not require us to postulate or infer a belief or a desire hidden away in the other person's mind. (Gallagher and Hutto, 2008, 20)

Specifically, based on work from Trevarthen (1979; Trevarthen and Hubley, 1978) they argue that we predominantly understand others through primary and secondary intersubjectivity. Primary intersubjectivity is the idea that we directly perceive other people *as people* and can directly perceive their goals and intentions.

> In seeing the actions and expressive movements of the other person one already sees their meaning; no inference to a hidden set of mental states (beliefs, desires, etc.) is necessary. (Gallagher and Hutto, 2008, 22)

In other words, the whole idea of mental states as something that is 'hidden' in the mind is to be rejected. This means that we do not need to engage in any theorising or simulation in order to indirectly access someone's mental states. Secondary intersubjectivity builds on primary intersubjectivity, but in secondary intersubjectivity children are able to go beyond the person-to-person interaction and consider also the pragmatic context of the situation. This is required, for example, for joint attention, where the child and the interaction partner jointly attend a third object.

Mindreading accounts are not unsympathetic to the idea that there might be something like primary intersubjectivity, which allows children to appreciate others as persons before they are able to engage in mindreading (Gopnik, 1993b; Gopnik and Wellman, 1992). However, IT goes further than this. They argue that strategies such as primary intersubjectivity are not only ontologically primary, but also remain so throughout life:

> Primary intersubjectivity is not primary simply in developmental terms. Rather it remains primary across all face-to-face intersubjective experiences. (Gallagher and Hutto, 2008, 22)

On this view, these processes of directly perceiving the mental states of others, both in their behaviour and through interaction, are our primary means of understanding others. Mindreading is a little – if at all – used strategy of social cognition.

To this, it can be objected that while it may be the case that we are able to perceive at least some mental states of others, it is highly questionable whether this is true of all mental states. It is notable that while mindreading accounts such as ST and TT usually focus on the attribution of mental states like beliefs, much of the discussion in interactionist accounts is oriented around emotions or pains. For example, they claim that I can directly perceive that my child is sad, or that the bus driver is angry. For such mental states with clear physical manifestations, it is much more plausible that we might be able to directly perceive these mental states.[9] It is much less clear that the same can be said about beliefs. The claim that we can directly perceive mental states is limited, therefore, leaving room for mindreading to play an important role.

---

9 Although recently even the assumption that there is a distinct pattern of physical expression for emotions has come under criticism (Feldman Barrett et al. 2019).

This is acknowledged by some of the proponents of IT, although they do not consider theorising or simulation as the decisive means for attributing mental states to others. For example, Hutto (2004, 2008, 2009) has famously argued for narratives as an important component of social cognition (referred to as Narrative Practice Hypothesis or NPH). He argues that early stages of social cognition are constituted by primary and secondary intersubjectivity. While these strategies remain in use throughout life, they are supplemented by narratives allowing for a richer attribution of mental states to others. Although this might be considered an alternative to TT and ST because it advocates a different structure, in which social information is processed and maintained, it is still an account of mindreading in the sense that it allows for attribution of mental states to others (Wolf et al., under review). Gallagher and Hutto (2008) point out that NPH still differs from mindreading accounts as the focus is less on the attribution of mental states per se as the narrative is structured predominantly around behavioural and situational aspects:

> [S]eeking a narrative understanding of the other's reasons is not a matter of characterizing the other's 'inner' life – if this is understood as a series of causally efficacious mental states. What we are attempting to understand is much richer; it is the other's reasons as they figure against the larger history and set of projects. (Gallagher and Hutto 2008, 33)

I agree that behavioural, historical, and situational aspects play an important role in social cognition and that social cognition cannot be reduced to attribution of mental states independently of the situational context. However, these should not be seen merely as alternatives for mindreading but as important components for enriching mindreading (Wolf et al., under review). For example, I can use historical information to inform my mindreading (e.g. attributing fear in the presence of a spider if I have the background knowledge that the person has arachnophobia). Similarly, the situational context will constrain, which mental states I attribute to someone. I will return to this point in more detail when discussing Andrews (2012) pluralist account below.

It is worth noting that the FBT itself is not committed to any form of the unobservability thesis. Although the FBT did arise in the context of predominantly TT accounts, the task itself is, at least in principle, not committed to any specific account of social cognition. All the task requires is for the child to observe a situation and then predict the behaviour of the other person. *How* they do this is not specified by the task; children might be solving the task by theorising or simulation, similarly, however they might also directly perceive the mental state in question and what they are going to do next.

However, the criticism of IT goes further and is explicitly directed against the methodology of the FBT. The heart of their criticism of traditional mindreading accounts is that these mindreading approaches do not adequately consider the interactive aspect of our understanding of others. In everyday life, we are not mere observers of others but actively engage with people. This opens up new avenues of understanding.[10] This criticism is explicitly extended to the FBT, which as a non-interactive task, in which the child takes the role of a detached observer, inherits the problems from the non-interactive theorising it originates from.

> Consequently, the experimental data [from the FBT] provide no genuine insight into the true range of children's false-belief understanding and fail to say what role such understanding might play in children's ability to make sense of others in more natural and less restricted interactional settings... At most, such tests tell us something about the onset of children's, still fairly basic, third person mentalizing abilities. (Hutto, 2009, 225–226)

While there are some interactive versions of the FBT, such as the active helping behaviour paradigm (which will be considered in more detail in Section 2.2.2) it is true that the majority of FBTs use third person observational situations to test belief attribution. Can we show that such third person mindreading abilities are important for social cognition? For a start, it seems clear that we engage in both directly interactive and third person observational activities that require understanding of others (Wolf et al, under review). There are several instances, in which we depend on third person observation, for example, a teacher must be able to observe children playing in the playground and predict the children's behaviour to some extent. When attending a lecture, I can look around the room to gage how other members are finding the lecture. It should also not be neglected that we do a lot of thinking about others when they are not present. So I might wonder what my friend who lives in another country thinks about the current political situation, or about how my mother will react to the gift that I will give her for her birthday in two weeks. Finally, we live in an increasingly digitalised society where there are fewer direct interpersonal interactions. Instead, we have a lot of communication via instant messages or email, where the cues that would normally provide the basis for direct perception of mental states are absent.[11] What these examples are intended to highlight is that social cognition is an incredibly

---

10 See also Butterfill (2013) for an account of how interaction can open up new avenues of understanding on a non-interactionist account.
11 For a more detailed discussion of paradigmatic cases of social cognition where mindreading is required and arguments why mindreading is a central strategy of social cognition, see Wolf and Coninx (2021) and Wolf et al. (under review).

diverse phenomenon. While direct perception in interactive settings may form an important part of our social understanding, there are many situations, in which social cognition is required in a non-interactive setting. In other words, while interactionists are right to criticise an exclusive focus on the observational stance within the mindreading literature, they seem in danger of committing the same error themselves in terms of a one-sided focus on interactions. Just as interactionists criticise TT and ST accounts for simply assuming that the third person case is basic and can be extended to second person interactive contexts, it can be objected that interactionists are wrong to assume that the strategies from the second person interactive context can be used to cover the third person 'decoupled' context (de Bruin and Kästner, 2012).

The interactionist might object here that although we do engage in third person observational mindreading, the direct interactive understanding is the basic one. Understood as a developmental claim this may be true, but it is unproblematic for a mindreading account. On the mindreading account, we can accept that social cognition originates in direct interaction. We can even allow that mindreading develops from a more basic social cognition arising out of direct interaction. All that is required is that social cognition extends beyond direct interaction. As long as this is the case, mindreading presents an important development in social cognition, allowing increasing flexibility beyond the immediate context. Therefore, the focus on the observational stance need not be a problem in the FBT as it is precisely this developing ability of social cognition that is detached from the immediate interactive situation, which we are interested in.

The Pluralist Critique of Mindreading

As we saw in the previous section, the interactionist approach encountered problems because it neglected the third person perspective too much. Pluralism seems to be a good way of dealing with this. On the one hand, it acknowledges that much of our understanding of others takes place in an interactive context where the mental states of the other person can be directly accessible to us. On the other hand, we can keep mindreading as a strategy that is important for a more flexible, complex and less situation bound means of understanding others. There are two central ways, in which pluralism differs from the above-mentioned interactionist accounts. Firstly, pluralism does not reject mindreading altogether. We have a number of strategies, which we make use of in social cognition, one of which can be mindreading. Secondly, pluralism widens the scope of alternatives to mindreading to include (amongst others) also prediction of behaviour based on the situation, stereotypes, behaviour scripts and generalisations over past behaviour (see Andrews (2017) for an overview of the different strategies thought to underlie social cognition).

While I am sympathetic to the general pluralist approach, a number of prominent pluralist accounts substantially restrict the role of mindreading (e.g. Andrews, 2012, 2017; Fiebich, 2015, 2019; Fiebich and Coltheart, 2015; Fiebich et al., 2017; but see Newen, 2015, Spaulding, 2018, and Westra, 2018 for recent accounts in the pluralist spirit that do not restrict the role of mindreading). While mindreading is not rejected entirely by these pluralists, on their view it only plays a subordinate role as a strategy that is rarely used and unreliable. In other words, mindreading is used only when all other strategies have failed. In this section, I will look at some of the arguments why mindreading is only a subordinate strategy and argue that these do not undermine the importance of mindreading and – importantly for our current purpose – do not undermine the importance of the FBT. Concerning the importance of the FBT, it should also be noted that neither Fiebich et al. nor Andrews, both of whose accounts I focus on in the following, actively deny the relevance of the FBT for the study of social cognition. Both in fact draw on findings from the FBT in their accounts (e.g. Fiebich, 2015), with Andrews (2017) explicitly suggesting that mindreading might not be the sole strategy children use in the FBT. The FBT might therefore be a useful tool for testing the different strategies children use across different situations and how these develop. I respond to their views because their rejecting of the centrality of mindreading in social cognition might be thought to undermine the research with the FBT and not because they themselves reject the paradigm.

I will begin by looking at the account of Anika Fiebich (2015, 2019; Fiebich and Coltheart, 2015; Fiebich et al., 2017). The main claim in her account is that – in principle at least – there is no default strategy of social cognition (Fiebich, 2015, 2019). This is unproblematic. A closer examination, however, reveals that Fiebich does think that there are some strategies, which we use more than others and are more central to social cognition. This falls out of her account on which strategy of social understanding we use and when, where she argues that we use whichever strategy suffices for the situation and requires the least effort (Fiebich, 2015, 2019). Mindreading, as most cognitively demanding strategy, will therefore only be used when all other strategies have failed, with direct perception and behaviour scripts being much more frequently used.

> In general, pluralist approaches contend that third-person mental state attributions that may involve theory or simulation do not lie at the heart of everyday social understanding and often come into play peripherally in ambiguous or unfamiliar contexts that make individuals puzzles about the other person's behavior... Other factors such as trading sec-

ond-person narratives; being sensitive to environmental contexts, norms, habits, social conventions; and having knowledge of character traits of familiar individuals are far more central. (Fiebich et al., 2017, 210)

As a more demanding strategy, mindreading would only be used in those situations, in which the other strategies fail or are not available. For example, we might resort to mindreading if predictions according to other strategies fail or if the strategy cannot be employed because, for example, we are faced with a novel situation, which we do not have adequate scripts for yet.

I will respond to this below after having also laid out Andrews' account, which largely overlaps with Fiebich's rejection of mindreading as a core strategy of social cognition. For now, however, I want to note that how cognitively demanding mindreading is seems to me to be an open question. While it is true that mindreading should be considered a sophisticated skill that children only acquire later than other strategies of social cognition, it is less clear whether, once acquired; mindreading really is that cognitively demanding. It is worth bearing in mind that, regardless of complexity, a process can come to be automatized through training (Logan, 1997; Suddendorf and Whiten, 2003). For example, the movements required for swimming are initially complex and require conscious control. Once practiced, however, much of the movement process becomes automatized. It is therefore too simple to argue that just because mindreading is initially cognitively demanding that it cannot become automatized. The literature on the automaticity of mindreading generates mixed results (Low et al., 2016). It seems possible that at least certain types or aspects of mindreading might be automatic and less demanding. In any case, the worry that mindreading might be a rarely used strategy because it is cognitively demanding does nothing to undermine research on mindreading. Even if it is not the most common strategy, the special interest in it may be justified precisely because it is a high-level activity.[12]

Andrews' (2012, 2017) pluralism has two components: firstly, in common with all pluralists, she argues that we have a variety of strategies underlying social cognition. Secondly, she emphasises that social cognition can have different

---

[12] This is not to say that the mindreading developed by children who pass the explicit FBT should be seen as the pinnacle of achievement in social cognition. Undoubtedly there is much development still to follow (see Apperly, 2011; Osterhausand et al., 2016). However, it does appear that several of these more advanced abilities concern more sophisticated application of mindreading (such as higher order mindreading (Boscoand et al., 2014; Miller, 2009, Osterhaus et al., 2016, Perner and Wimmer, 1985) or mindreading in more complex scenarios (Happé, 1994; O'Hare et al., 2009).

purposes. She highlights in particular a distinction between action prediction and action explanation. She argues that mindreading is only really used for action explanation and not action prediction. While she therefore allows a role for mindreading within social cognition, this might be considered problematic for two reasons. Firstly, action explanation only really needs to take place when action prediction has failed. In this sense, the result is similar to Fiebich's account where mindreading only occurs when the other strategies have failed. Secondly, the FBT, which I am primarily interested in here, usually asks for action prediction rather than explanation (although see H. Wimmer and Mayringer (1998) and Amsterlaw and Wellman (2006) for examples of FBTs requiring action explanation).

Andrews gives four reasons why mindreading is not usually used for action prediction.[13] The first is that in our day-to-day interactions we are not conscious of attributing mental states to others, [14] therefore mindreading would have to be automatic, which there is no empirical support for. As noted above, the empirical literature concerning the automaticity of mindreading is, as of yet, unclear. Andrews cites evidence from Apperly et al. (2006; Back and Apperly, 2010) in favour of the view that mindreading is not automatic. Apperly's own position, however, is that at least some forms of minimal mindreading are automatic (Apperly, 2011; Low et al., 2016), as there is evidence that another person's false belief can under some circumstances interfere with an adults performance (Schneider, Nott, and Dux, 2014; van der Wel et al., 2014). Apperly's explanation of these mixed findings are that there are two systems of mindreading: one being an automatic and fast 'minimal mindreading' system, the other non-automatic but more flexible mindreading system (Apperly and Butterfill, 2009). It may be that Andrews does not consider minimal mindreading as a proper form of mindreading, but this would require further argument.

Secondly, Andrews thinks that we do not regularly use mindreading to predict the behaviour of others as mindreading is a very unreliable strategy. The mapping from mental state to behaviour and *vice versa* is not one to one.

> The relationship between observable behavior and the propositional attitudes that presumably cause behavior would be too complex to allow for timely, much less accurate, prediction of behavior. (Andrews, 2017, p119)

---

13 This discussion is based on Andrews (2017). The same points are elaborated in Andrews (2012).
14 Andrews specifically mentions beliefs in this regard.

The objection that the search space for mental states might be too large is not new. However, there might be ways of avoiding this problem by allowing that the situation itself or our aims in the situation might constrain the search space. We do not just see behaviour in isolation, but behaviour taking place within a particular context. For example, the mental states I attribute to someone running away from a fire are very different to those I attribute to someone running towards the finishing line in a race, even if the behaviour removed from the context might be the same. Admittedly, this still leaves a wide range of mental states, which could be attributed (e.g. in the case of the fire there might be fear, the desire to protect oneself, the belief that one might die), but in most everyday situations we probably do not need a such a fine-grained attribution of mental states in order to suitably predict someone's behaviour and interact with them.

Furthermore, it seems that this problem is not specific to mindreading, but also applies to many of the other strategies that Andrews does think play an important role in the prediction of action such as behaviour scripts or inferences based on past behaviour (Wolf and Coninx, 2021). Except in some stereotypical and tightly constrained situations such as established greetings or procedures, the relationship between past behaviour and future behaviour is also likely to be complicated. Similarly, behaviour scripts are also likely to be complicated in their application outside of some few heavily regulated behaviours such as ordering food in a restaurant or paying at the till. We do use behaviour scripts, but these are flexible in their application and subject to considerable variation. For example, I might have a restaurant script but I must frequently deviate from this depending on the specificities of the restaurant I am visiting. For example, I might be offered a drink with my bill in some restaurants and not others, or it might happen that the food that I ordered was out. What these examples are intended to bring out is that behaviour scripts are not always simple rules to be followed, but must allow for complexity and variation in line with the complex world we face.

Additionally, Westra (2020) has pointed out that we currently do not have any good means of measuring the reliability of mindreading except for very broad and basic mindreading. Measures such as the FBT task test at best the ability to attribute very general mental states to others in situations where the context is usually strongly constrained. These tests are therefore far removed from assessing the accuracy of everyday mindreading, where there are multiple situational influences and complexities. Additionally, many tests of accuracy of mindreading depend on a comparison with introspection. For example, one way in which we might measure the accuracy of mindreading is to compare the attribution of mental states to a person with their self-report. The accuracy of introspection, however, has also been questioned (Nisbett and Wilson, 1977; Schwitzgebel, 2008). Westra therefore argues that the claim that mindreading is unreliable is not based on any strong empirical evidence and we simply do not know whether mindreading is reliable or not. That a complex task leads to errors is unsurprising and not necessarily an indication of an unreliable ability per se and, as I have argued, other strategies of social cognition are not immune to these problems.

Thirdly, Andrews thinks that the early developmental data provide us with some reason for thinking that we do not actually need mindreading in order to predict the behaviour of others. If we think that failure in the explicit FBT shows that children do not yet understand beliefs then their early abilities to predict or anticipate the behaviour of others must be explained in an alternative manner.[15] The matter of what exactly the early success in the implicit FBT shows is controversial. Similarly, it is also controversial whether failure in the explicit FBT must be attributed to an absence of mindreading. Finally, even if one grants this, one could still object that just because children are able to predict the behaviour of others before learning mindreading, this does not mean that as adults who are capable of mindreading we do not make use of this strategy. Andrew's point seems to be that the abilities of young children show that we do not *need* mindreading in order to predict the behaviour of others, but for this argument to work, it would need to be the case that 3-year-olds who do not yet pass the explicit FBT are as good or at least almost as good as we are at predicting the actions of others. The explicit FBT seems to provide clear evidence against this – there are some cases, namely those, in which false beliefs are involved, where children are worse at predicting the behaviour of others. To provide a stronger response to the argument from Andrews, however, it would be good to have some more naturalistic and more varied studies of children's ability to predict the behaviour of others as compared to adults. Even if children before the age of 4 predict the behaviour of others without mindreading, as adults who are capable of mindreading we might nonetheless make use of this strategy to allow for more specific or more flexible predictions of behaviour. Finally, it is worth noting that this argument seems to be specifically against *belief* attribution as a means of predicting behaviour, rather than against mindreading in general. Our concern here is primarily with belief attribution, as this is what the FBT aims to test, so concerns about the importance of belief attribution are relevant for us. Nonetheless, it is an open question to what extent this type of criticism could cast doubt on the importance of mindreading more generally.

---

15 I return to the question of how to interpret the findings from the implicit FBTs in Chapter 3.

Andrew's final argument against mindreading for predicting actions builds on the previous objections highlighting the shortcomings of mindreading and makes the claim that we have alternative strategies, which are not subject to the same shortcomings as mindreading. Above, I have already highlighted some cases where particular alternative strategies can suffer from the same problems as mindreading. The point to note about this is that all strategies, when used alone, are subject to limitations and uncertainty. I might read the situation wrong and therefore use the wrong behavioural script. I might misapply a stereotype. It is only through integrating the use of different strategies and using a variety of strategies *in conjunction* that we are able to successfully understand interact with other people (Wolf et al., under review). In this context mindreading might even be considered especially notable as 1) it is less tied to a particular situation (unlike e.g. behaviour scripts), and 2) mindreading is used especially in those situations where prediction using alternative strategies may have failed, i.e. in explanation. Contra to Andrew's account, this action explanation, however, is not independent from prediction, as we are able to *learn* from this in order to make predictions in the future. Mindreading might therefore be especially important in learning and adapting predictions of behaviour to new situations.

Within this, belief attribution can be thought of as particularly central to the ability to detach understanding of others from a given situation. While Gallagher and Hutto (2008) may be right in noting that often we share a perspective, belief attribution is crucial especially in those situations where we do not share a perspective. This gives our ability to act and interact a significant amount of flexibility, which we would not otherwise have. Moreover, as argued before, situations in which we do require these special abilities are not that rare and form a central part of our everyday social cognition.

Finally, when considering the plurality of strategies used for social cognition, it is not only important to see that we often use multiple strategies in parallel for a given situation, but that we often actively combine them and use them in conjunction. For example, I might have historical knowledge not only of past behaviour, but also of past mental states that resulted from a situation: I do not just know that Annie cried last time that she lost her teddy, but also that losing her Teddy made her sad. This sadness could result in a number of behaviours, allowing me to interpret and predict her behaviour more flexibly: I might predict that she will not only cry, but also that she will not sleep because she has done this in previous situations where she was sad independently of losing the teddy. Similarly, I might have stereotypes not only about people's behaviour, but also about their mental states. For example, I might associate particular beliefs about abortion with the stereotype of a Catholic.

What the discussion in this section was intended to show is that mindreading is an important strategy of social cognition, both in its own right and as a strategy, which is combined with other strategies of social cognition. None of this is in conflict with the basic pluralist idea that in social cognition we make use of multiple strategies to make sense of others. However, on this pluralist picture mindreading plays an important role and is not to be neglected.

1.3 Conclusion

In this chapter, my aim was to defend the FBT as an important test of social cognition against recent criticisms. As we saw, the reasoning behind the FBT was that the FBT is a particularly stringent test of belief attribution. By testing belief attribution, it tests the ability to attribute mental states to others (mindreading), which is thought to be a central ability within social cognition. Many recent criticisms have focused especially on criticising the idea that mindreading really is a central component of social cognition. While it is clear that mindreading cannot be the sole basis of social cognition and that we make use of a plurality of strategies for understanding others, I have argued that mindreading nonetheless plays an important role within social cognition. This is especially so because mindreading specifically allows for long-term understanding of individuals and allows for more detachment from a specific situation. The FBT tests this ability and therefore measures an important developmental step in social cognition.

Having therefore defended the FBT and mindreading, I will now move on to consider the evidence from the FBT in the following chapter. The central element of focus will be the contrast between the findings from the implicit and explicit FBTs with the aim of determining the nature of the phenomenon we are trying to explain.

2 The False Belief Task – A Developmental Sketch of the Paradox of False Belief Understanding

In the previous chapter, I defended the role of mindreading and the false belief task (FBT) in research on social cognition. In this chapter, I will focus more closely on the different types of FBT and how they give rise to the paradox of false belief understanding. The FBT is the central task used in the literature to assess children's belief understanding. These tasks assess children's belief understanding by testing whether they can attribute beliefs to others and use this to predict their behaviour. There are two main types of FBT: the classic explicit FBT, which children tend to only pass at the age of 4, and the implicit FBT, which much younger infants already seem to pass. This generates a puzzle for developmental researchers: if infants already pass the implicit FBT, why do they nonetheless fail the explicit FBT till the age of 4? My aim is to make clear the empirical findings, which give rise to the paradox of false belief understanding, thereby clearly identifying the phenomenon requiring explanation. This will form the basis of the new account of the paradox of false belief understanding developed in Chapter 4.

In this chapter, I will first provide an overview of the different types of FBT, beginning with the explicit FBT (Section 2.1.) and then the implicit FBT (Section 2.2.). Within the implicit FBTs, I argue for a distinction between looking behaviour and active helping behaviour based implicit FBTs. This means that within the paradox of false belief understanding we not only need to account for the two stage difference between performance on the implicit and explicit FBT, but a three stage development of false belief understanding (see also Newen and Wolf, 2020). Finally, I consider and argue against some objections, which might be raised against this three stage developmental sketch.

2.1 The Explicit False Belief Task

The FBT has occupied a central position in the mindreading literature for more than the past 30 years. With "explicit FBT", I mean the classic, direct, verbal FBT of the kind that was first used by Heinz Wimmer and Josef Perner in 1983. In their "Maxi Task", children watched a doll, Maxi, place his chocolate in the green cupboard. He then goes out to play and while he is gone, his mother moves the chocolate from the green to the blue cupboard. Maxi then returns and the

https://doi.org/10.1515/9783110758610-006

child is asked, "Where will Maxi look for his chocolate?" The change of location is the central element of the task, as it introduces a distinction between Maxi's belief and reality and therefore allows researchers to determine whether the response is based on Maxi's belief. This task has since been replicated many times and the reliable finding is that children systematically fail this task till the age of 4 (Wellman et al., 2001), saying that Maxi will look for the chocolate in the blue cupboard (where they know the chocolate actually is), as opposed to the green cupboard where Maxi initially placed the chocolate. It is important to note that they make this systematic error, even though they correctly remember where Maxi initially placed the chocolate, so their problem does not lie in being unable to remember what happened.

We can distinguish between three different types of explicit FBT:

1. **Change of location FBT.** As we saw in the Maxi task above, this task introduces a distinction between where the agent believes an object to be and where it actually is. The agent therefore has a false belief about the *location* of an object, and children must predict the agents' behaviour based on this. (See also Baron-Cohen, Leslie, and Frith, 1985)

2. **Unexpected contents FBT.** In this task, the agent has a false belief about the *identity* of the *contents* of a container. A typical example of this is the 'smarties task' (Gopnik and Astington, 1988; Perner, Leekam, and Wimmer, 1987), inducing the belief that this box contains smarties. The box is then opened and they are shown that the box actually contains pencils. The box is closed again and children are asked what someone who has not seen the contents will think is in the box. One advantage of this paradigm is that it can also be used to test children's understanding of their own false beliefs by asking what *they themselves* initially believed was in the box (Gopnik and Astington, 1988).

3. **Appearance Reality FBT.** In this task the agent has a false belief about the *identity* of an object, which is usually induced by means of a deceptive object such as a sponge painted to look like a rock (e. g. Flavell, Flavell, and Green, 1983; Gopnik and Astington, 1988). Children are shown the object that looks like it is a rock. They are then invited to interact with the object so that they realise it is actually a sponge. They are then asked what another person, who is newly shown the object, will think it is.

These different variations of the FBT correlate well with each other and the finding that children fail this task till the age of 4 persists across the different paradigms (Wellman et al., 2001). This suggests that the problem children have with the FBT is not just specific to either object location or identity, but is a general problem with attributing false beliefs.

Moreover, it is notable that findings from the explicit FBT are very robust and persist over a number of variations in the task set-up within the three types of explicit FBT. For example, we get the same pattern of results regardless of how the scenario is presented (e. g. whether the scene is acted out with puppets, human actors or whether they are shown a film). Similarly, the findings persist whether the story includes deliberate deception or not (Wellman et al., 2001). As a result, many researchers concluded that there was some significant cognitive change occurring in children at the age of 4 in terms of their ability to understand the beliefs of others (Apperly and Butterfill, 2009; Gopnik and Wellman, 1992; Perner, 1991; Wellman et al., 2001; for a notable exception see Leslie, 1987; Scholl and Leslie, 2001).

These findings were challenged by the advent of the implicit FBT, which seems to provide evidence of some earlier belief understanding in infants. It is these tasks, which I turn to next.

2.2 The Implicit False Belief Task

The implicit FBT has gained considerable prominence in the literature following Onishi and Baillargeon's (2005) seminal paper, in which they pioneered a fully non-linguistic implicit FBT, which even 15-month-old infants were able to pass. While the explicit FBT makes use of a direct, question and requires a direct linguistic response, the implicit FBT measures false belief understanding more indirectly making use of indirect measures such as eye gaze. Unlike the explicit FBT, where we find a high level of coherence across the different variations of the task, the implicit FBT appears to be a less unified group (Rakoczy, 2017; Grosse-Wiesmann et al., 2017). In this section, I will provide an overview of the different versions of the implicit FBT. Based on this I will argue that we can identify two different stages of belief understanding as measured by the implicit FBT.

2.2.1 Looking Behaviour Based Implicit False Belief Task

The paradigmatic versions of the implicit FBT inspired by the work of Onishi and Baillargeon (2005) use looking behaviour as an indirect measure of belief understanding. There are two different versions of this task: firstly, tasks that make use of looking duration as a measure of surprise and, secondly, tasks that measure anticipatory looking. Both versions make use of a set up very similar to the explicit FBT. For example, children see an object being hidden in a blue box and, while the other agent is looking away, the object is moved from the blue box to the green box. However, unlike in the explicit FBT, children are not asked a direct question to which they must respond.[1] In the looking duration implicit FBT, looking duration for the belief congruent event (i.e. reaching for the object in the blue box) and belief incongruent event (i.e. reaching for the object in the green box) is measured and compared. It has been found that infants at 15 months and younger look significantly longer at the belief incongruent event than the belief congruent event (Onishi and Baillargeon, 2005; Song and Baillargeon, 2008; Surian et al., 2007).[2] This longer looking is interpreted as evidence of surprise, which would indicate that infants did form an expectation of the other person's action based on their beliefs, even though they still provide an incorrect response verbally. In the anticipatory looking paradigm, children receive a signal, which they learn indicates that the other person will reach into one of the two boxes. Children's first look towards the boxes once the signal sounds is measured. A number of studies have found that upon the sound children look first towards the blue box where the agent last saw the object (Southgate et al., 2007, see also Clements and Perner, 1994; He et al., 2012; Scott et al., 2012). In these tasks children seem to anticipate that the agent will act in accordance with their false belief as opposed to reality. This again appears to be in conflict with the findings of the explicit FBT, where children predict that the other person will act according to reality. There is even evidence of concurrent success in the implicit FBT while failing the explicit FBT i.e. in children showed correct anticipatory looking while giving the wrong response to a direct verbal question (Clements and Perner, 1994; Garnham and Ruffman, 2001; Low, 2010).

Looking behaviour based implicit FBTs have not only made use of the change of location paradigm, but also the unexpected contents (He et al., 2011) and a deceptive objects paradigm requiring understanding of object identity (Scott and Baillargeon, 2009), thus showing that the competence shown by infants in the implicit FBT is flexible over a wide range of false beliefs, similar to their performance across different versions of the explicit FBT (Scott, 2017).[3]

---

1 One exception here is the anticipatory looking FBT by Clements and Perner (1994) where children were asked a direct question. It has been suggested that this question may be the reason why children only passed this task at age 3 and not earlier, as has been shown in other anticipatory looking paradigms.

2 Kovács et al. (2010) were even able to show evidence of calculation of others' beliefs in 10-month-old infants. This paradigm, however, varied slightly from the traditional false belief story used in the other FBTs.

3 But see Low et al. (2016) for a critique of these studies.

There are, by now, many versions of these looking behaviour based tasks, which pertain to show some robustness and flexibility of the phenomenon (see Scott, 2017, and Scott and Baillargeon, 2017 for recent reviews and Barone et al., 2019 for a more critical meta-analysis of recent implicit FBTs). Despite this, there are issues concerning how to interpret the evidence from these studies. Is the looking behaviour sufficient to show that children are attributing beliefs, or is their behaviour based on some more basic understanding? This is especially true of the looking duration studies, where the longer looking may indicate surprise in light of belief attribution, but could also be due to some other novelty of the observed scene (Heyes, 2014a). This invites low-level alternative interpretations of findings from the implicit FBT, which do not suppose early levels of belief understanding. Such accounts will be discussed in more detail in Section 3.4. Here evidence from more 'active' behavioural paradigms may be useful in providing clearer evidence, as behavioural responses are more direct and therefore easier to interpret that something like merely longer looking. It is these studies, which I turn to in the next section.

Before doing so, it should be noted that there is a further concern about the replicability of these findings. While the findings from the explicit FBT replicate well and seem robust, this has not always been the case for findings from the implicit FBT (Kulke and Rakoczy, 2018; Poulin-Dubois et al., 2018). I will return to discuss issues of replication in Section 2.3.3.

2.2.2 Active Behaviour Paradigms

Aside from looking behaviour paradigms, there are also paradigms, which require a more active behavioural response from the child. Active behaviour paradigms are useful because they appear to provide more direct evidence for infant's belief understanding. Furthermore, these tasks often feature a strong interactive element, which may make them closer to some of our everyday cases of social understanding.[4] While they are often characterised as another form of the implicit FBT, I will argue that the demands posed by this task are actually quite different and therefore competence in the active helping behaviour paradigms should be seen as distinct from the competence displayed by infants in the looking behaviour-based tasks.

---

4 See Chapter 1 (especially Section 1.2.2.) for a discussion of the role of interaction within social understanding.

In order to show this, let us consider the one of the first active helping behaviour studies by Buttelmann, Carpenter and Tomasello (2009) pertaining to show belief understanding in 18-month-old infants. This paradigm makes use of the independent finding that children show helping behaviour from the age of 14 months in non-FBTs. Buttelmann et al. extend this to the FBT with a set-up very much like that of the standard change of location FBTs. Children were introduced to an experimenter who placed a toy into one of the boxes in front of them and left. These boxes could be locked by means of a pin. The children knew how to unlock the boxes while the experimenter did not. While the experimenter was gone, the toy was moved from the one box to the other and the boxes were locked. The experimenter then returned and tried to open the box, in which he had initially placed the toy. Children were encouraged to "help him". The key idea behind this experiment is that children must consider the experimenter's false belief concerning the location of the object in order to help appropriately. That is to say, that they must consider that the experimenter (falsely) believes the toy to be in the initial box in order to conclude that he is trying to retrieve the toy when trying to open this now empty box. Indeed, what Buttelmann et al. found was that in the false belief condition 18-month-old children 'helped' the experimenter by retrieving the toy from the other box. Crucially, in a true belief condition where the experimenter also observed the change in location, children 'helped' the experimenter by opening the empty box that the experimenter was trying to open. This is important as it shows that children did not just retrieve the toy by default, regardless of the beliefs of the other person. It is this difference in behaviour between the two conditions, which provides evidence that children take into account the beliefs of other people to guide their helping behaviour. Buttelmann et al. also carried out the same experiment with 16-month-olds, but found the evidence here to be less conclusive.

Buttelmann et al. (2015) also extended this active helping behaviour paradigm to a version of the appearance reality task. In this, the child saw the experimenter playing with a toy duck. The experimenter then left and while she was gone, it was revealed that this duck was actually a brush. This 'duck-brush' was then placed on a shelf. When the experimenter returned, she tried to retrieve the object, which, however, was out of her reach. At this point two unambiguous objects (a brush and a cat) were revealed behind a screen and the child was asked to help get the experimenter the object he wants. Buttelmann et al. found that when the experimenter did not know about the real identity of the ambiguous object, children retrieved the duck. However, in the true belief condition where the experimenter also knew that the object was actually a brush, children retrieved the brush. This task is significant not only because it not only indicates a flexibility in the active helping behaviour paradigm, but also because these findings suggest that children's performance cannot be explained purely in terms of an understanding of knowledge and ignorance without actually representing the perspective of the other person. While the initial findings from the 2009 study might be explainable in terms of the child only tracking the experimenter's ignorance, the findings from the F. Buttelmann et al. (2015) study seem more difficult to explain in such a manner. That the child retrieves the duck in the false belief condition where the experimenter does not know that the duck is actually a brush is more difficult to explain in terms of a rule like "if they are ignorant, then they get it wrong."

While the Buttelmann et al. (2009) study is perhaps the most famous and can be seen as the paradigmatic task based on an "action-based usage of theory of mind skills" (Knudsen and Liszkowski, 2012, 673), there are a number of other tasks, which also fall into this category. For example, Southgate et al. (2010) carried out an 'active helping study', in which children were asked to retrieve a 'sefo' toy. Here children needed to consider the other person's false belief in order to correctly disambiguate, which toy was referred to in order to retrieve the correct toy. Similarly, Knudsen and Liszkowski (2012) carried out a communicative pointing study, in which they showed that children selectively pointed to warn the other person only in cases when there was an undesirable object at the location where the person (falsely) believed their toy to be. These paradigms similarly provide evidence of an early form of sensitivity to the beliefs of others.

2.3 Three Stages in the Development of Belief Understanding

While these kinds of active behavioural paradigms are often considered to simply be another form of the implicit FBT akin to the looking behaviour based paradigms, I want to argue that they are actually different in a number of ways. In order to do so, it is worth considering for a moment what it means for an FBT to be an implicit FBT.[5] How do we distinguish between implicit and explicit FBTs? There is no clear agreement on this in the literature, with some authors concentrating on the nature of the response required (e. g. De Bruin and Newen, 2012) and others concentrating on the nature of the question posed (e. g. Scott, 2017). One popular means of differentiating between implicit and explicit FBTs is in terms of spontaneous vs elicited response tasks. While the explic-

---

5 The term 'implicit FBT' originates from the early study using looking behaviour by Clements and Perner (1994) who hypothesised that there may be an implicit belief tracking system which underlies the early success. The term has since become the most common in the literature and is often used without commitment to two processing systems as I have been doing so here.

it FBT is an elicited response task, at least the looking behaviour based FBTs are spontaneous response tasks. The active helping behaviour task, however, seems to pose a problem for this distinction as it is an elicited task (Priewasser et al., 2018). Even though children are not directly asked what the other person believes, they do receive a prompt to help. Therefore, on this criterion the active helping behaviour task appears more like the classic explicit FBTs.[6]

Due to this, Baillargeon et al. (2010) have proposed two kinds of implicit FBT: spontaneous response FBT and indirect elicited response FBT. However, it is also debatable to what extent the active helping behaviour task is indirect. Firstly, there is some reason for arguing that the active helping behaviour task is direct as the children act directly *in order to help the experimenter* (Carruthers, 2013; Priewasser et al., 2018). Secondly, if we consider the active helping behaviour task indirect, some of the tasks ordinarily considered explicit FBTs such as the original Maxi task might, on these criteria, count as indirect as the question they are asked is about Maxi's behaviour and not directly about her belief.

A final criterion often used to distinguish between implicit and explicit FBTs is the role of language.[7] Here too the active helping behaviour task seems problematic. Admittedly, these tasks do not require a verbal response from the child, but language is involved in setting up the task and eliciting the response from the child. In this sense too, therefore the task remains similar to the explicit FBT.

Considering these differences between the requirements of the different implicit FBTs, Vierkant (2012) has proposed a distinction between different kinds of implicit false belief understanding based on the different kinds of responses required from the child. He points out the difference between a child who "has transformed his behavioural repertoire" and one that "has the right looking patterns [but] will at most display very moderate differences in her behaviour" (Vierkant, 2012, 142). Neither child has an explicit belief understanding as they still give the incorrect response verbally to the question of where Maxi will look for her chocolate, but the kind of implicit belief understanding displayed by the children is very different.

---

6 A close look at Buttelmann et al.'s (2009) study in fact reveals that they considered both children who helped spontaneously upon the return of the experimenter and those who helped following a prompt. This seems to suggest even more strongly that the task fails to fit into the neat distinction of elicited vs spontaneous FBT. Other implicit FBT studies, however, such as Southgate et al.'s (2010) 'sefo study' experiment, clearly make use of elicited response FBT.

7 As noted above, there was also language involved in Clements and Perner (1994) anticipatory looking experiment and it has sometimes been suggested that this was the reason why they only found successful performance at age 3 and not in younger children.

While I do not want to deny the importance of active behaviour in distinguishing between the different kinds of belief paradigms, I want to highlight a further difference between the looking behaviour based tasks and the active helping behaviour task which, I will argue, is of critical importance. Passing the looking behaviour based FBT requires the child to take the perspective of the other person. The active helping paradigms, on the other hand, go further than this in that they require the child to relate the other perspective to their own knowledge of the situation (Newen and Wolf, 2020). For example, in order to correctly anticipate where the other person will reach in the anticipatory looking paradigm of Southgate et al. (2007), the child only needs to be able to determine the perspective of the other person. Where the toy actually is is not relevant to passing the task. In fact, this information about reality may actually hinder passing the task by confusing the child. In the active helping behaviour paradigm by Buttelmann et al. (2009), however, the child must consult the other person's perspective in order to determine the goal (retrieve the toy), but then must also consider *the reality of where the toy actually is* in order to help appropriately.[8] Similarly, in the Knudsen and Liszkowski (2012) paradigm, the child must understand the agents goal of wanting to retrieve the toy in order to predict where the agent will go. They must then, however, make use of their knowledge of reality – i.e. that there is actually an object that the agent wants to avoid in that location – in order warn the agent. Finally, in the 'sefo' paradigm of Southgate et al. (2010) the child must use the agent's perspective in order to understand, which object is being referred too, however they must then make use of their own perspective in order to retrieve the correct toy. The active helping behaviour paradigms therefore provide first evidence of children being able to make use of two different perspectives within the context of one task. This is something, which is not required by the looking behaviour based studies.

This need to switch between perspectives, which, as I will show, is a crucial difference between the different kinds of implicit FBTs. Action may play an important role in the development of the ability to switch between perspectives. It is therefore unsurprising that many of these tasks, which require perspective switching, are active behavioural tasks. One exception to this is the study by Moll et al. (2017), who showed that 2.5-year-old children express suspense when watching another person approach reality with a false belief. In this study, children watched a puppet show, in which the 'Cookie Monster' had placed his cookies in a box. After he had left, the number of cookies in the

---

8 Priewasser et al. (2018) have criticised this interpretation of the Buttelmann et al. (2009) study, as will be discussed in more detail in Section 2.3.2).

box was reduced so that the Cookie Monster had a false belief about the number of cookies in the box. Moll et al. recorded children's facial expressions in this false belief condition and compared them to a true belief condition, in which the Cookie Monster saw the cookies being taken out of his box.[9] Moll et al. found that children showed significantly more tension and suspense in the false belief than in the true belief condition, suggesting that children realised that the Cookie Monster had false expectation concerning the contents of the box, which was about to be revealed. In this case, the response is a spontaneous emotional one, and not a controlled behavioural response. This might suggest that relating of perspectives is not only possible in the context of action. It must also be noted, however, that these children are already 2.5 years old, while the children in the Buttelmann et al. (2009) and Southgate et al. (2010) studies were considerably younger. It is therefore still possible that the initial ability to switch between perspectives is set up in the context of action.[10]

Based on this I therefore suggest stages of belief understanding, which lie on a gradual developmental continuum (see also Newen and Wolf, 2020):

1. Early sensitivity to other's beliefs (15 months and possibly younger)
2. More sophisticated usage of early sensitivity to belief (e. g. as required by the active helping behaviour task) (approx. 18 months)
3. Explicit ToM involving explicit belief attribution (4 years)

The reason for positing these three stages in the development of belief understanding is that tasks pose different demands and children pass these tasks at different stages in their development. While very young infants have been shown to pass implicit looking behaviour based versions at the age of 15 months (Onishi and Baillargeon, 2005),[11] they do not pass the active helping behaviour paradigms till the age of 18 months. Similarly, children do not pass the explicit FBT till the age of 4.

There are two points to be made about this sketch. Firstly, although I have identified three developmental stages, I do not want to argue for development as a set of discrete steps. Evidence from a longitudinal study by (Baker et al., 2016) provides some indication that the development of children's performance

---

9 As well as this 'Reduction Story', there was also a 'Breaking Story', in which the protagonist's object was broken, a 'Replacement Story' where the object was exchanged, and a 'Deconstruction Story' where the protagonist's Lego construction was taken apart. No differences between reactions to the different stories were reported.

10 I will consider the role of action in more detail in Section 4.3.4 when developing my account of the development of false belief understanding.

11 Or even at 10 months (Kovács et al., 2010).

on the explicit FBT over time is gradual and varies significantly between individuals. I therefore endorse a continuous development view, where these three stages highlight significant achievements on a continuum. This development is influenced by both cognitive maturation and situational factors. This means that the age, at which children pass these types of tasks might be more flexible, not only because of individual differences in cognitive development, but also because the situational context the child is exposed to may have an important impact both on cognitive development and performance on the FBT, as I will discuss in more detail in Chapter 3 (especially Section 3.2.) and Chapter 4.

Secondly, I do not mean to commit myself to the view that the early sensitivity shown by success on the implicit FBT should be classed as an understanding of belief. For now, I leave it open whether this should be considered belief understanding or a precursor of such understanding (for example in terms of belief-like states). I will return to this question in Chapter 4 (Section 4.4.) where I argue that at least the early sensitivity shown in the looking behaviour based tasks is probably insufficient to be classed as belief understanding. Nonetheless, this early sensitivity is at least an important precursor to belief understanding.

There are a number of objections that might be made against this sketch, which concern in particular the interpretation of the active helping behaviour paradigms. I address these in the next section. What is important for my purposes is this intermediate stage where children are already able to consider different perspectives to some extent, but which is still clearly distinct from the level of performance at age 4 when passing the explicit FBT. I will first consider some general concerns about the interpretation of the active helping behaviour paradigm as a distinct stage of belief understanding. I will then look in more detail a recent experiment by Priewasser et al. (2018) pertaining to provide evidence for an alternative teleological interpretation of the active helping study by Buttelmann et al. (2009). On this interpretation, passing the active helping behaviour task does not require perspective taking (Section 2.3.2.). I then consider more general concerns about the replicability of the implicit FBTs and the active helping behaviour paradigms in particular (Section 2.3.3.).

2.3.1 General Objections

The first objection against the developmental trajectory outlined above is that, given the similarities between the explicit FBT and the active helping behaviour, why not just consider the active helping behaviour task a variant of the explicit FBT. The reason for this distinction between explicit FBT and active helping behaviour FBTs is that children are able to pass active helping behaviour FBTs much earlier than the explicit FBT, which they pass only at 4 years of age. We are therefore still faced with the question of why children fail the explicit FBT till age 4, while being able to pass the active helping behaviour based task at 18 months.

It has been suggested that one reason why the active helping behaviour paradigm is easier than other versions of the FBT is that children do not have to resist the 'pull of the real' in this task. In order to succeed in the false belief condition, children do not have to ignore where the object really is and instead make use of reality in order to retrieve the toy. Even in the active helping behaviour paradigm, however, the child does have to resist the pull of the real in order to determine the goal of the other person (Newen and Wolf, 2020): the experimenter returns and looks into the empty box so the child must inhibit the knowledge that the toy is actually in the other box in order to realise that the experimenter is looking for his toy. Furthermore, while the child may not need to resist the 'pull of the real' when retrieving the toy in the false belief condition, they do have to inhibit the pull of the real in the control true belief condition where they should not retrieve the toy (Newen and Wolf, 2020). In this condition, the experimenter has seen the toy being moved but nonetheless go to open the now empty box. The child needs to open the empty box, ignoring the fact that the toy is now in the other box. It does seem that resisting the pull of the real – in this case specifically the pull of the actual location of the object – is something children struggle with, given that especially the true belief condition from the Buttelmann et al. (2009) study has proven hard to replicate. For example, Priewasser et al. (2018) replicated Buttelmann's finding that the children retrieved the toy in the false belief condition. However, they also sometimes did so in the true belief condition leading to a performance, which did not differ from chance. Nonetheless, the findings from Buttelmann et al. (2009) suggest that at least under some circumstances children can resist the "pull of the real".

An alternative objection to the three-stage view outlined above is to question whether there really is a distinction between the first and second stages of belief understanding. In particular, while the demands of the tasks might be different, it might be objected that the evidence that children really start to pass these tasks at different points and therefore provide evidence of two different stages of belief understanding is scant. The age difference between stages 1 and 2 is not that large and it is not clear that younger children cannot pass the active helping behaviour task. Even if it were the case that they cannot do this, this failure may be due to other reasons such as limitations in their motor control or an only rudimentarily developed helping behaviour.

My response to this is two-fold. Firstly, it should be noted that it is the best interpretation of the data we have so far. In particular, my claim is that we have evidence of children being able to switch between perspectives to some extent from the age of 18 months through the active helping behaviour studies. We lack evidence suggesting that children are able to do this at an earlier point. Of course this alone does not mandate claiming children do not have this ability at an earlier point (although see Southgate (2013) for some theoretical arguments for this view). I do not, however, see any positive reason at this moment for attributing this ability to them either. Furthermore, given the issues there have been in replicating some of the active helping behaviour studies – which have largely only been successful in 3-year-old children – there is some reason to be sceptical that successful performance on these active helping measures will be found at an earlier stage.

Secondly, with regards to alternative limitations preventing them from passing the task, it should be noted that children do engage in helping behaviour at the age of 14 months already (Warneken and Tomasello, 2007), while their helping behaviour on an FBT has only been shown at 18 months, with some inconclusive evidence at 16 months.

Finally, what is crucial for the development of my account is that there is an early ability to relate perspectives to each other as shown by the active helping behaviour task. Although I will develop my account as a three stage account in Chapter 4, should there be evidence that children are already able to relate perspectives from the start and that there is no distinction between stages 1 and 2, this would not be fatal for my account as long as this initial stage already consists of a (limited) form of being able to use different perspectives within the context of one task (see Section 4.3.4.).

2.3.2 Teleology – An Alternative Interpretation of the Active Helping Behaviour Study?

In outlining the developmental trajectory, I leaned heavily on the active helping behaviour paradigm developed by Buttelmann et al. (2009). Recently, concerns about the interpretation of this study have been raised. Priewasser et al. (2018) have argued for a new 'teleological' interpretation of the data from the paradigm, according to which children attribute goals to the experimenter based on the objective facts of the experimental set-up, rather than the experimenter's beliefs. On the teleological view in question here, young children do not understand behaviour in terms of the person's mental states, but in terms of objective facts. (Perner and Roessler, 2010). In other words, children view people as acting for objective reasons in order to reach goals. So, for example, when Maxi comes in looking for his chocolate, it is objectively good for him to find his chocolate. Moreover, the reason why Maxi goes to the cupboard is because that is where his chocolate is, and not because that is where he *believes* his chocolate is. Importantly, what this basic form of teleology does not allow for is consideration of differences in perspectives. Applying this teleological framework to the active helping behaviour paradigm, Priewasser et al. argue that in the false belief condition, children attribute the goal of retrieving the toy to the experimenter when he returns based on his previous interest in the toy. In the true belief condition, on the other hand, the experimenter seems as if he has lost interest in the toy and therefore they do not attribute the goal of retrieving the toy to him.

It should be noted that I am not objecting to the teleological account in general. In particular, I am very sympathetic to the idea of a teleology *in perspective*, which is an extension of the basic teleology that has been developed by Perner et al. (2018) as an alternative to the classic belief attribution accounts. Teleology in perspective differs mainly from the classic accounts in that the focus is mainly on different perspectives on the world, rather than the other person's mental states, which is compatible with the account I will develop later. However, what Priewasser et al. (2018) aim to show in this paper is that the findings of the active helping behaviour task can – and should – be explained in terms of teleology simpliciter, that is to say teleology without perspective taking. It is this, which I will object to.

In order to distinguish between Buttelmann et al.'s mentalistic interpretation and the teleological interpretation, Priewasser et al. carried out an active helping behaviour paradigm with three boxes instead of two. This allowed them to have two more conditions in addition to the original true belief and false belief conditions. The original true belief and false belief conditions were the same as in Buttelmann with the exception that there were three boxes instead of two, but only two of them were used. For example, the experimenter placed his toy in box A, the toy was then moved to box B and the experimenter returned and tried to open box A. In the new conditions, the procedure was the same as in the original experiment except that the experimenter attempted to open box C (which had previously not been in play) as opposed to box A (where the toy had initially been placed). Crucially, as Priewasser et al. (2018) argue, the new false belief condition allows us to distinguish between the two interpretations of the original experiment. According to Buttelmann et al.'s mentalist interpretation, children know that the experimenter believes that the toy is actually in box A, therefore their attempt to open box C should not be interpreted as an attempt to retrieve the toy.

According to BCT's theory children will know that E2 [the experimenter] believes that the toy is in box A and should therefore show the same preference for the box E2 is trying to open. (Priewasser et al., 2018, 75)

According to the teleological explanation, on the other hand, children should expect the experimenter to have the goal of retrieving his toy when she returns: based on the experimenter's behaviour it seems that the toy is the experimenter's toy, which he has a noted interest in.

Children – according to our hypothesis – are fairly sure that the agent is coming back to look for her toy. However, she goes to the wrong box. (Priewasser et al., 2018, p76)

Therefore, on the teleological interpretation, children should show a preference for opening the box the toy is actually in, not the box, which the experimenter is trying to open.[12] To summarise, according to the mentalistic interpretation, children should attempt to open box C in the new false belief condition, while on the teleological interpretation children should open box B. Priewasser et al. (2018) found that in this new false belief condition, more children still retrieved the toy from box B. Priewasser et al. conclude that this provides strong evidence in favour of their teleological interpretation over Buttelmann's mentalist interpretation.

There are some issues with this experiment, however.[13] Firstly, Priewasser et al. were only partially successful in replicating the original Buttelmann et al. (2009) study. They were able to replicate the false belief condition and show that children did retrieve the toy. However, unlike in the original study, children also sometimes retrieved the toy in the true belief condition leading to a level of performance, which did not differ from chance. Taken as a whole, the interpretation most supported by the data is that children have a tendency to retrieve the toy regardless of the condition. Quite plausibly it might have been that the toy was so interesting to the children that they simply retrieved this without any regard to what the experimenter was doing, that is to say without any regard to either mentalizing or teleology. One way of avoiding this prob-

---

12 Concerning the new true belief condition both the mentalistic and the teleological account make the same prediction, namely that the child should look in box C (i.e. the empty box which the experimenter is trying to open). As this prediction is the same for both I will not focus on this further here.

13 See also Newen and Wolf (2020) for a similar criticism of the experiment.

lem would be to have a second independent toy in each box such that the interest in each box is equal from the perspective of the child.[14]

Secondly, the introduction of the third box may have made the task more confusing for children. Priewasser et al. (2018) themselves note this, in particular that "the use of three boxes flattened the distribution of chosen boxes" (74). That is to say that there seemed to be an increase of "error responding" (74) or, as Priewasser et al discovered, a preference for the central box (which was also where E2 looked first upon re-entering the room). In order to exclude this error Priewasser et al. excluded all central box responses and considered only responses towards the left or right box, leaving them with the very small sample size of only 8 children. The presence of the third box seemed to have an impact already in old true and false belief tasks where the third box was merely present and not used in the task. Given the effect in the true belief and false belief conditions in increasing children's error and uncertainty, it does not seem implausible to suppose that children might have been even more overwhelmed in the new true belief and false belief conditions where the third box was actively involved in the procedure. Therefore, Buttelmann et al. could suppose that the children were so overwhelmed by the three-box set-up that they *did not know that the experimenter believed the toy to be in box A*. They might have forgotten this information in the confusion and therefore acted based on the most salient information in the situation: where the toy actually is.[15]

As a result, while the findings from Priewasser et al. (2018) do not support my view, they also do not speak clearly against a mentalistic reading of the findings from the active helping behaviour paradigm and do not show that children do not consider different perspectives in this task. Nonetheless, it must be noted that their alternative interpretation of the findings of the original Buttelmann et al. (2009) paradigm indicates that it would be possible to pass this specific task without needing to make use of the other person's perspective and therefore, pending further evidence to adjudicate between the different interpretations, this task is unable to provide conclusive evidence of children's ability to make use of two different perspectives within the context of one task. This, however, does not challenge the general argument for distinguishing between the three stages of development as the Priewasser et al. study focuses specifically on the Buttelmann et al. paradigm while, as I discussed above, there are a range of different studies such as that by Knudsen and Liszkowski (2012),

---

14 Although this may also make the task more demanding and thereby cause further problems for the children.
15 See also Baillargeon et al. (2018) for a similar critical discussion of the findings from the Priewasser et al. (2018) study.

which also provide evidence of an early ability to combine different perspectives (see Section 2.3).

2.3.3 Replication Worries

A further worry to be addressed is the question of replication. Issues concerning replication are rampant in psychology. While the findings from the explicit FBT seem to be on solid ground and replicate well, there have been growing concerns about the replicability and hence the validity of the findings of infants early success in the implicit FBTs (Dörrenberg, Rakoczy, and Liszkowski, 2018; Kammermeier and Paulus, 2018; Kulke and Rakoczy, 2018; Kulke et al., 2018; Kulke, von Duhn et al., 2018; Poulin-Dubois et al., 2018). This is true of both the looking behaviour based paradigms and the active behaviour paradigms. In the discussion below, however, I will focus mainly on the active behavioural paradigms as they have been subject to the most criticism and are the most central to my later argument.

At first sight, the fact that the findings from the implicit FBT are now being called into question again might seem surprising. After all, there are by now over 30 studies that pertain to have shown infants success on these tasks (Baillargeon et al., 2018; Scott, 2017). Furthermore, there have been some animal studies also replicating some of the basic implicit FBTs based on looking behaviour (Kano et al., 2017) as well as active helping behaviour (Buttelmann et al., 2017). However, most of implicit FBT studies showing early success in infants have been conducted by the same research groups with other groups struggling to get the same results (Poulin-Dubois et al, 2018). For example, Buttelmann's active helping behaviour paradigm has at most been partially replicated in other research groups (Kulke and Rakoczy, 2018). It is perhaps to be expected that some research groups have more experience and expertise with these paradigms and therefore achieve better results. Research with young children is difficult. Experimenters must maintain children's interest and attention on the task in order to obtain results, which is something not to be taken for granted. Nonetheless, replicability is one of the fundamental elements of science. Should it turn out that even following close consultation with the original experimenter paradigms, the results still prove difficult to replicate, this would be concerning and cast considerable doubt on the initial findings.

It should be noted, however, that although there often is contact with the original experimenters prior to replication attempts, the fewest of the replication studies are actually direct replications, which use exactly the same set up as the original paradigm. Most replications are conceptual replications, which follow the same general idea of the original study but change some elements (Kulke and Rakoczy, 2018). It is therefore possible that some of the failed replications are due to these changes in the task. This is emphasised by Rubio-Fernández (2018), who points out that many of the implicit FBTs are "fragile paradigms" (317) that are sometimes hard to replicate as success depends on many task factors. In other words, conditions must be optimal to achieve success. However, this itself does not undermine the significance of the findings of the implicit FBT: even if children are only able to succeed in the implicit FBT under optimal conditions, this is still significant.

However, this explanation is limited and can only be used up to a point. If children's performance is conditional on factors down to the colour of the clothes the experimenter wears, we might worry that the paradigm now wears too thin. More specifically, if the implicit FBT paradigm is to be truly useful, we need to have predictions under what conditions children are able to succeed and why they fail. Currently, there are responses following failed conceptual replications as to how these replication attempts differ from the original study and how this led to failure (Baillargeon et al., 2018; Rubio-Fernández, 2018). But this still needs to be systematized further in order to be able to determine in advance whether a replication should succeed or not. This, however, is beyond the scope of this book and may require further empirical investigation and analysis of successful and failed replications.

Ideally, what we need are large-scale direct replications to test the replicability of these tasks, as well as conceptual replications to test the boundaries of these paradigms. There is some work being done in this direction (e.g. the Many Babies Project[16]), but this is still in its early stages. Furthermore, it is unclear that this will bring a final resolution to the conflict given, as we have seen, that small changes in the experimental set-up may lead to significant changes in performance. What may initially have been set up as a direct replication may in fact turn out to merely be a conceptual replication.

So, how to proceed in light of this uncertainty? Should we leave all discussion of the development of children's belief understanding till we have the data from these large-scale replications? I think this would be a mistake. As I have stated above, I am sceptical whether even these large-scale replications will be able to resolve the issue. It is also worth noting that the question of whether infants already have an understanding of ToM was already a live one before the advent of the implicit FBT (Leslie, 1987, 1994). If it does turn out that none of the data from the implicit FBT replicates, this does not show that children

---

16 https://manybabies.github.io/

lack belief understanding till the age of 4. It may simply be that the implicit FBT is a poor means of testing this early belief understanding. This is not to say that the evidential base for belief understanding from the implicit FBT is completely irrelevant. The findings from the implicit FBT are an important basis of the view that there is at least an early sensitivity to the beliefs of others. However, the findings from the implicit FBT are not the *only* basis for attributing such sensitivity to infants. There are alternative sources, which lend support further to this, such as evidence from perspective taking and pretend play, which I discuss at a later point in this book.

To conclude, for the purposes of this book I will make use of the empirical evidence from the implicit FBTs to back up my arguments, assuming that the basic phenomena are genuine. However, I will also provide theoretical motivation for the critical intermediate stage of the account I develop in Chapter 4. Finally, I will consider evidence from the literature on perspective taking (Chapter 5) and pretend play (Chapter 6) to further back up my arguments.

2.4 Conclusion

Summing up, in this chapter I argued for a three stage development of belief understanding, beginning with an early sensitivity for belief displayed in the looking behaviour based FBTs, to a more sophisticated usage of this early sensitivity as tested by the active helping behaviour tasks and finally to an explicit attribution of beliefs. I also looked at some objections to this three stage developmental trajectory, making clear why I think the performance on the active helping behaviour paradigm should be distinguished both from the early sensitivity to belief, which the looking behaviour based tasks tap into, as well as the later explicit belief attribution shown in the explicit FBT. I also acknowledged, however, that the evidence concerning the implicit FBTs is still somewhat tenuous at this point, given the recent worries about replication. What is crucial for me is the intermediate stage at which children already need to be able to relate different perspectives to each other to some extent. In the next chapter, I will consider previous accounts in the literature that aim to explain the paradox of false belief understanding, before presenting my own account of the three-stage development of belief understanding in Chapter 4.

3 Theories of Mindreading – The Role of Cognitive and Situational Factors in Belief Understanding

In the previous chapter, I reviewed the evidence from the false belief task (FBT) and we saw that young infants are able to pass some forms of implicit FBTs while they systematically fail explicit versions of the FBT till age 4. This gives rise to the paradox of false belief understanding. I argued that between passing implicit looking behaviour based FBTs and passing explicit FBTs there is an intermediate stage characterised by the active helping behaviour paradigms that children pass at around 18 months.

How can we explain this development? In the literature, we find two different factors that are used to explain the difference in performance. On the one hand, there are accounts, which explain the paradox of false belief understanding in terms of some cognitive development (*cognitive factor*). This means that the explicit FBT places higher cognitive demands on the child than the implicit FBT and therefore some further cognitive development is required in order to pass the explicit FBT. On the other hand, there are accounts that argue that the difference in performance is largely due to *situational factors*.[1] That is to say that they focus on the situational context of the FBT and argue that there are certain features of the explicit FBT, which make it harder for children to pass. For the purpose of this discussion, I take situational factors to be a broad category ranging from elements of task set up and elements influencing the child's experience beyond the task itself. As such, my understanding of situational factors is broader than that of some other accounts in the literature such as Westra (2016) who is more specifically focused on the pragmatics of language as a situational factor impacting performance on the FBT. My core claim will be that in order to provide a full account of the development of belief attribution in the context of the paradox of false belief understanding, we must consider both situational and cognitive factors *and how they interact* in development. While this at first sight may seem trivial, this has so far been neglected in the literature where we find that accounts usually focus predominantly on only one factor. Before entering into the discussion of the individual accounts (Section 3.3. and Section 3.4.), I will briefly clarify what is meant by cognitive

---

[1] The distinction between cognitive and situational accounts was first introduced in Newen and Wolf (2020, Sections 1.1 and 1.2).

https://doi.org/10.1515/9783110758610-007

(Section 3.1.) and situational factors (Section 3.2.) and how they feature in the literature.

3.1 Cognitive Factor

In the literature, much of the focus has been on the cognitive factor. While everyone agrees that there is some kind of cognitive development, which underlies the shift in performance on the explicit FBT at age 4, there is considerable disagreement on the nature of this development. On the one hand, we find the early competence accounts, according to which children have an early and possibly innate ability for mindreading (Baillargeon et al., 2010; Baron-Cohen et al., 1985; Carruthers, 2013, 2016; Leslie, 1987, 1994; Leslie et al., 2004; Scholl and Leslie, 2001). The challenge for these accounts is explaining why, despite this early competence, children nonetheless fail the explicit FBT. The answer, on these accounts, is that children lack some form of inhibition ability or executive function that is required in order to pass the explicit FBT. It is the development of these *domain general cognitive abilities* that explains the shift in performance at age 4. On the other hand, according to late competence accounts children lack belief understanding till they pass the explicit FBT at age 4. It is a change in the *domain specific ability* to represent and reason about beliefs that explains the change in performance at age 4. These accounts face the reverse challenge of the early competence accounts, namely explaining why much younger infants are nonetheless able to pass the implicit FBT.

The two-systems account developed by Apperly and Butterfill (2009) might be thought to lie between both camps. Based on the two systems distinction from Kahneman (2003, 2011), Apperly and Butterfill argue that there is one early and quick "cognitively efficient but limited and inflexible system" (system 1) (Apperly and Butterfill, 2009, 966) which is sufficient for the implicit FBT only. The explicit FBT requires the second, "highly flexible but cognitively inefficient" (Apperly and Butterfill, 2009, 966), mindreading system (system 2), which only comes online at around age 4. For the purpose of this discussion, however, I will group the two systems with the late competence accounts as they share the view that infants do not yet have a full understanding of belief and that there is some domain specific cognitive development required in order to attain this understanding at age 4. In the debate between early and late competence accounts, what is at stake is whether passing the implicit FBT requires belief attribution or not and therefore, whether passing the implicit FBT shows belief understanding.

The debate between early and late competence accounts runs orthogonal to the cognitive/situational account discussion. For example, while Baillargeon et al. (2010), Leslie (1987, 1994; Leslie et al., 2004, 2005) and Carruthers (2013, 2016) put forward what I class as cognitive accounts because their explanation of development makes reference only to changes in internal cognitive organisation; Helming et al. (2016) and Westra (2016) argue for 'pragmatic' accounts, that is to say they argue that the situational context plays an important role in explaining infants failure in the explicit FBT. The same distinction is found in late competence accounts, although the boundaries are somewhat less clear here. For example, Perner's accounts (both the meta-representation account of Perner (1991) and the more recent mental files accounts from Perner and Leahy (2016)) are cognitive accounts that consider only internal cognitive reorganisation. Heyes (2014b, 2018), on the other hand, focuses almost exclusively on the role of situational factors. A summary of the layout of the literature about situational and cognitive accounts and how these relate to early and late competence accounts is shown in Table 3.1.

Although I will structure my discussion of the accounts according to the early and late competence distinction, as this is the dominant means of classification in the literature, it should be noted that my aim in this chapter is not to argue for either an early or a late competence account. Much of the debate between the early and late competence accounts rests on the question of whether children have a concept of belief or not, and at what point in development they can be said to have attained this. As I made clear in my first chapter, this is not my primary concern. There remains a question of how to explain the difference in performance between the implicit and the explicit belief, regardless of whether the behaviour children show in the implicit FBTs should count as proper belief understanding already or only as a precursor. Furthermore, it is unclear what it means to have a concept of belief and what the criteria for having such a concept might be (Apperly, 2011), which further complicates answering the question of whether children have a concept of belief or not. Finally, unless one is committed to some version of modularity, it is also a complicated issue to determine whether a development really is domain specific or domain general. At what point does a change in inhibitive power that substantially changes the way beliefs are processed become a domain specific change in belief processing? I will therefore not argue in favour of either an early or late competence account here. I will, however, return to these issues again after developing my account of the development of belief understanding in Chapter 4 (Section 4.3.5.) where I suggest some criteria to help disentangle the issues.

Table 3.1: Systematic overview of the main accounts of the paradox of false belief understanding (taken from Newen and Wolf, 2020, Table 1, 721)

	Cognitivist Account	Situational Account	Cog/Sit Combined Account
Nativist	Theory of Mind Module — Baron-Cohen (1995)	Pragmatic Account — Helming et al. (2016)	
	Response Account — Baillargeon et al. (2010)	Pragmatic Development Account — Westra (2016)	
	Triple Mindreading — Carruthers (2013, 2016)		
	Theory of Mind Mechanism (ToMM) — Leslie (1987, 1994); Leslie et al., 2004, 2005)		
Neutral	Differential Task Demands View — Rubio-Fernández (2013)		Situational Mental File Account — Newen and Wolf (2020)
Empiricist	Two Systems Account — Apperly and Butterfill (2009); Butterfill and Apperly (2C13)	Submentalizing/cognitive gadgets — Heyes (2014b, 2018)	Child Scientist – Theory Revision — Gopnik (1993a); Gopnik and Wellman (1992, 2012); Wellman (2014)
	Behaviour Rules and Meta-representation — Perner (1991); Perner et al. (1987)		
	Mental Files — Perner et al.. (2015); Perner and Leahy (2016)		
	Dual Systems Association Account — De Bruin and Newen (2012)		

3.2 Situational Factor

There are two ways for situational factors to enter into the performance on the FBT. Firstly, situational factors can influence performance on the FBT itself. For example, performance is improved if the task is set up such that the object is removed from the scene entirely or the child herself does not know where the object is (Mascaro and Morin, 2015; Mascaro et al., 2017; Wellman and Bartsch, 1988). Furthermore, Lewis et al. (2012) showed that children's understanding of other people's beliefs actually improves if another person is added to the scenario who also observes the change in location. Similarly, there is evidence that children's performance improves if it is emphasised that "you and I both know where the chocolate is" before asking them where Maxi will look for her chocolate (Hansen, 2010). In a highly influential recent study, Rubio-Fernández and Geurts (2013) also provided evidence that children's performance on the FBT improves if the perspective of another person is highlighted.[2] These studies were all carried out with the explicit FBT, but one interpretation of this evidence that is popular especially amongst the early competence accounts is that similar situational factors are at work in the implicit FBT, making these tasks easier for infants than the classic explicit FBT. This means that children's performance on the FBT is ultimately determined by the situational factors of the task, which can either support or impede performance.

Secondly, situational factors can influence performance on the FBT more indirectly. The child's context, beyond the set-up of the FBT, influences performance on the task. For example, it has been found that children with older siblings perform better on the FBT, passing it slightly earlier than children who do not have older siblings (Perner et al., 1994; Ruffman et al., 1998, see Cassidy et al. 2005 for an overview). Similarly, children whose mothers make use of more mental state talk perform better on the FBT (Ruffman et al., 2002). This is an example of the indirect effect of situational factors, where situational factors impact on cognitive development hence allowing for better performance.

Like cognitive development, it can hardly be denied that situational factors influence children's performance on the FBT. The role that situational factors play within development, however, are very much subject of debate. Central matters of debate are whether situational factors are sufficient to explain children's failure on the explicit FBT till age 4 and whether situational factors influence

---

2 Although the findings from Rubio-Fernandez and Geurts have proven hard to replicate (Kammermeier and Paulus, 2018; but see Rubio-Fernández (2018) for a response). I return to discuss these studies and their interpretation in more detail in Chapter 4.

children's belief understanding itself or merely their performance on the task (i.e. whether situational factors influence children's actual understanding of belief, or whether they merely impact on their ability to exercise this ability). I will illustrate this using an example. There is a very famous study looking at false belief understanding in the early cohorts of deaf students learning the Nicaraguan Sign Language (Pyers and Senghas, 2009). This language was only developing, with that of the first cohort being less complex than that of the second. In particular, the first cohort did not have any mental state vocabulary. It was found that the first cohort performed significantly worse than the second cohort which did have mental state vocabulary, with the first cohort systematically failing the explicit FBT.[3] This suggests that exposure to language plays an important role for the development of belief attribution. This is further supplemented by findings that deaf children who are born into non-sign-language speaking households also show a delay in passing the FBT (Meristo et al., 2007; Peterson et al., 2005). In this case, the impoverished language input (situational factor) could either have impaired or delayed the *development of belief understanding*, or it could be that the lack of experience with belief discourse impaired their *understanding of the FBT itself* such that they fail the FBT even though they are, in principle, able to attribute beliefs to others (as suggested by Westra, 2016). Similarly, there are several studies providing evidence of cultural differences regarding when children first come to pass the FBT (Liu et al., 2008). Especially in countries where there is less mental state talk, children seem to be delayed in passing the FBT. However, it is unclear whether this delay is due to a delayed development of belief understanding, or whether the FBT is just more foreign to children in these cultures and they therefore do not understand what is being asked even though they are capable of attributing beliefs.

Having introduced cognitive and situational factors, I will now look at the previous accounts of the paradox of false belief understanding in more detail. My central claim in this chapter is that we require an account that considers the role of both cognitive and situational factors in conjunction across development in order to provide an adequate account of the paradox of false belief understanding. So far, this has not been sufficiently acknowledged in the literature. At first sight, this claim might seem trivial and something that all accounts endorse on some level. According to cognitive accounts, some form of cognitive development is required in order for the children to pass the additional demands of the explicit FBT. But where do these additional demands come from? Presumably from the set-up of the explicit FBT, i.e. from situational factors. Similarly, situa-

---

3 Both cohorts were adults at the time of testing.

tional accounts argue that it is situational factors that cause children's failure in the explicit FBT. Eventually, however, these obstacles are overcome, presumably due to some form of cognitive development.[4] The claim, therefore, is not that a combined account of situational and cognitive factors is incompatible with previous accounts. Many accounts would be compatible with a combination and this is sometimes even explicitly acknowledged (Helming et al., 2016; Westra, 2016). Rather, my point of criticism is that none of the previous accounts systematically considered the interrelation between both factors. Accounts usually focus on one or the other factor, providing a developmental story focusing on either situational or cognitive factors, while leaving open the role of the other (Newen and Wolf, 2020). It is this independent consideration, which I object to in this chapter.

3.3 Early Competence Accounts

Early competence accounts tend to be modular views according to which children have a domain specific module to process mental states which is innate (Carruthers, 2013; Leslie, 1987, 2002; Scholl and Leslie, 2001) or comes online very early in development (Baillargeon et al., 2010). In this section, I will consider some of these prominent early competence accounts and argue that they fail to adequately consider the role of situational factors. I will then look at some of the recent attempts to integrate situational factors within early competence accounts and will argue that while these are right to consider the importance of situational factors, situational factors are still insufficiently integrated with cognitive development in these accounts.

Alan Leslie is one of the prominent defenders of an early competence account (German and Leslie, 2001; Leslie, 1987, 1994; Leslie et al., 2004, 2005). He argues that children have an innate Theory of Mind Module (ToMM) which allows them to understand both their own mental states and those of others. He defends this view in light of evidence of children's early pretence (Leslie, 1987, 2002) and, more recently, their success on the implicit FBT (Wang and

---

4 One exception here is Westra's (2016) pragmatic account. He argues that children fail the explicit FBT due to lack of experience with belief discourse. Here, therefore, there is scope for a purely situational account where it is just further experience with belief discourse that allows children to improve their performance. Westra himself, however, does not endorse such a specifically pragmatic account and does think that there is cognitive development in the form of increased executive function and inhibition abilities that also underlies the change in performance in the explicit FBT.

Leslie, 2016) which, he argues, show that young children are already capable of belief attribution. Their problem in the explicit FBT, therefore, is not due to a lack of understanding of beliefs or an inability to attribute beliefs to others. Instead, he argues their failure is due to an insufficiently developed 'selection processor' which is required in order to select the correct response in the explicit FBT (Leslie et al., 2005). This selection mechanism depends significantly on being able to inhibit one's own perspective.

Baillargeon et al. (2010) also defend a version of the early competence account. They argue for a two systems account of belief understanding. However, unlike Apperly and Butterfill (2009) who make use of the two systems to make sense of the dichotomy in performance between implicit and explicit FBT, Baillargeon's second system is already in place by the time of passing the implicit FBT. Like Leslie, she argues that it is low inhibition abilities that prevent children from passing the explicit FBT, even though they already have sufficient belief understanding.

Although Leslie and Baillargeon differ in their accounts of how belief understanding comes about, their accounts are rather similar as to why children fail the explicit FBT, namely children have problems in response selection and inhibition. For our purposes, therefore, we can consider them together. There are at least two problems with these views. Firstly, they do not adequately account for the role of situational factors. I think, however, that this is a gap in the account, rather than a fatal objection. Roby and Scott (2016) have recently argued that although early competence views such as Baillargeon's cannot claim that experience plays a role for the development of the concept of mind and belief, it may nonetheless play an important role in learning the correct application of these concepts. Similarly, as we shall see later, Evan Westra (2016) similarly has shown that situational factors can be accommodated within an early competence framework. Therefore, there is room for acknowledging the role of situational factors within Baillargeon's and Leslie's account.

The second problem is more pressing. Both accounts rest on the idea that children's problem is that the explicit FBT requires children to exercise inhibition capacities while the implicit FBT does not. Specifically, children must inhibit their own perspective in order to give the correct response and it is here that children fail. It is unclear, however, why the explicit FBT requires these inhibitory skills while the implicit FBT does not (Newen, 2015). This is especially problematic given, as we have seen, many of the implicit FBTs are very similar to the explicit FBT in terms of their set-up. Leslie and Baillargeon et al. agree that in the explicit FBT, children must inhibit their own perspective, but why do they not need to do so in the implicit FBT? After all, in the implicit FBT they still have their own knowledge of where the object in question actually is which conflicts with the perspective of the other person. Why does the child's knowledge not require extra inhibition in the implicit FBT paradigms?

Southgate (2013) has put forward a view that might be helpful to consider at this point. She argues that young infants are able to succeed in the implicit FBT because they have a bias towards the perspective of others. She argues that children have an early ability to represent the perspective of others and indeed have a bias towards this perspective. Their own perspective is either not represented at all, represented in a different manner or is simply less salient than the perspective of others during the early months. This means that the implicit FBT is not very demanding on executive function as taking the perspective of another is the default position. The FBT only becomes difficult for children once their own perspective reaches salience. At this point, executive functions are needed in order to select the right perspective and these are not sufficiently developed until age 4.

While this would explain why perspective selection is not needed for the early implicit FBT, there are a number of problems with this view. Firstly, the findings from the active helping behaviour paradigm are problematic for this view. In the previous chapter, I argued that these tasks require both self and other perspectives. Hence, it is not sufficient to only represent the perspective of the other person. The child needs to access her own perspective too. On Southgate's view, this would require executive function in order to select the correct perspective and therefore children should only pass these tasks at age 4. As we saw, however, children show competence in these tasks at the age of 18 months already. Secondly, there are findings of simultaneous failure in the explicit and success in the implicit FBT. For example, Clements and Perner (1994) showed that 3-year-olds looked in the correct location in anticipation, but still gave the wrong response. This is also problematic for Southgate's view as it seems that there is interference from the own perspective in one case but not the other. Therefore, it seems that it cannot just be the case that the own perspective is not represented, allowing for success in the implicit FBT, as children fail the explicit FBT *at the same time* as passing the implicit FBT.

A different early competence view which provides an alternative account why the explicit FBT requires more executive function and inhibition abilities is that of Carruthers (2013). He argues that the explicit FBT is in fact a *triple mindreading task*. Children need to attribute mental states to the other person in order to determine what the other person will do, but this is not sufficient for the explicit FBT. In addition, they also require mindreading in order to interpret the question of the experimenter and in order to formulate their response. The problem children have in the explicit FBT therefore is not that they must engage in mindreading, but that they must engage in *triple mindreading*. It is this threefold demand that is too much for the early cognitive system of the child.

Here too, however, the active helping paradigms seem to pose a problem. For example, in the Buttelmann et al. (2009) paradigm, children are asked to "help him", an assertion which would require interpretation. Although the response required is not verbal, it is not clear to me why this behavioural response would require less mindreading than the formulation of a verbal response of naming the location.

Even leaving aside the problem posed by the active helping behaviour, this still does not dissolve the problems for the early competence accounts advocated by Leslie, Baillargeon and Carruthers, as the evidence for the role of executive function and inhibition abilities in passing the explicit FBT is mixed. While there is evidence that the explicit FBT correlates with executive function (Devine and Hughes, 2014; Mutter et al., 2006), Westra (2016) has noted that this correlation is usually not very strong and only explains a relatively small amount of the variance in performance on FBTs. Furthermore, there is also evidence that children from cultures with higher executive function scores do not pass the explicit FBT earlier, and in fact sometimes only pass the FBT later (Westra and Carruthers, 2017). This would suggest that lack of executive function could not be the full picture. What is required is some consideration of the situational factors that, as we know, play a role in belief attribution. In this sense, the first problem identified, namely the lack of consideration of situational factors, is actually related to the second problem: it is unclear why the implicit FBT requires these extra inhibition and executive function skills. To be clear, the problem is not that these accounts cannot accommodate the evidence of the effect of situational factors, but that their cognitive account itself would depend on a close analysis of the situational factors in order to explain why the explicit FBT is so much more demanding. Therefore, the lack of consideration of situational factors considerably weakens the cognitive account they develop.

There are two early competence accounts that consider the role of situational factors. These are Helming et al.'s (2016) Pragmatic Account and Westra's (2016) Pragmatic Development Account. I will consider each in turn.

3.3.1 Helming et al.'s Pragmatic Account

Helming et al. (2016) put forward an interesting 'pragmatic' version of an early nativist account. They interpret infants' early success in the implicit FBT as evidence of their belief understanding, and argue that success in the explicit FBT does not depend alone on understanding beliefs. The way the explicit FBT is set up places additional demands on the child, leading them to fail. In particular, what Helming et al. note is that by having an experimenter asking the question, "Where will Maxi look for his chocolate?", the explicit FBT introduces two perspectives for the child to consider. On the one hand, the perspective that the child shares with the experimenter, both of whom know where the chocolate actually is and, on the other hand, Maxi's perspective. Similar to Leslie (1994; Leslie et al., 2005) and Carruthers, (2013), Helming et al. argue that the problem lies not in computing the other person's perspective, but in selecting the correct perspective. Helming et al. differ from Leslie and Carruthers, however, in that they do not think that this is merely a matter of lacking inhibition abilities, but rather that there are elements of the task, which systematically bias the child in favour of selecting the perspective shared with the experimenter. There are two biases in particular which act on the child. First, the child has a bias towards helping the other person, and hence towards indicating the location where the object actually is (Cooperation Bias). Second, the question is posed to the child by an experimenter who shares the same perspective with the child – in particular, who also shares knowledge where the object actually is. As it is the experimenter who asks the question, Helming et al. argue that this biases children towards the perspective they share with the experimenter, hence leading them to give the wrong answer.

A problem with Helming et al.'s account, however, is that it is not adequately integrated with cognitive factors (Newen and Wolf, 2020). As noted above, this is a nativist account, so there is no need for an account of how children's understanding of belief develops, but we do need an account of how children are able to overcome their problems with the explicit FBT at age four. Presumably increased executive function and inhibition abilities (i.e. cognitive factors) play a role here, highlighting the need for a combined situational and cognitive factors account.

However, it is important to note that the issue lies not only in being able to inhibit a response, specifically also in being able to *select* the correct response. In other words, there are two components of executive function: one needs to not only being able to inhibit a response but also have some means of determining which the correct response is (M. Wimmer and Doherty, 2011). For example, on Helming et al.'s account, the problem lies not only in inhibiting the perspective shared with the experimenter, but in determining which perspective is the relevant one for the task (e.g. realising that the question is about Maxi's belief and not reality). This, once again, shows that cognitive and situational factors need to be considered together to provide an account of development. On the one hand, situational factors may highlight one perspective which is not relevant for the task and which must be overcome by a cognitive development in terms of situational factors. On the other hand, a child must learn to read a situation in order to determine which perspective is the relevant one for the task. The ability to read a situation therefore is foundational for correctly selecting which perspective to inhibit. This ability to read a situation to determine which aspects are important goes beyond the early situational triggering and might require some understanding of typical situations or scripts in order to realise that the belief of the other person is relevant. It is a more active process than the early, entirely passive triggering of a particular perspective due to situational factors and a certain level of cognitive development may be a prerequisite. The idea is still, however, that certain features of a situation are apparent and stand out to a more experienced mindreader that are not so apparent to a novice, in the same way that an experienced firefighter will notice different things about a burning house than a naïve bystander. Newen (2017) has also argued that there is good evidence that expertise can change the way a situation is perceived from the example of expert chess players. Expert chess players' perceptual experience is systematically enriched by their knowledge of chess, allowing them to perceive patterns that a novice would not see. This more nuanced receptiveness for situational factors in turn plays an important role in determining what should be inhibited (cognitive factor).

3.3.2 Westra's Pragmatic Development Account

Westra's (2016) Pragmatic Development Account aims to provide an answer to the question of why children struggle to give the correct response in the explicit FBT. He argues that children's failure in the explicit FBT is not due to a failure to understand the beliefs of others, but rather due to a systematic misinterpretation of the questions they are asked. This misunderstanding occurs because children are unfamiliar with belief discourse. That is to say, they do not appreciate the relevance of beliefs for conversation. Most of the conversations children experience are about reality and what *the case is* rather than about what other people *believe to be the case.* Therefore, they systematically misinterpret the question about Maxi's belief about the chocolate to actually be a question about the real location of the chocolate. In other words, Westra attributes children's early failure in the explicit FBT to a failure in the pragmatics of language. It is only once they gain more experience with belief discourse that they are able to correctly interpret the question they are being asked.

The advantage of this account is that it provides not only an explanation of why children fail the explicit FBT till age 4, but also why they are able to pass the task later in development, namely because they have gained the experience in belief discourse they were previously lacking to allow them to correctly interpret the question. The account also fits well with the evidence that situational factors such as maternal mental state discourse improves performance (Ruffman et al., 2002), or that task modifications which make more clear that the question is about what the other person believes and not about what really is the case improve performance (e.g. Hansen, 2010; Siegal and Beattie, 1991). Nonetheless, I think that the lack of consideration of cognitive development is problematic for this account for two main reasons (see also Newen and Wolf, 2020). Firstly, children's problems with the explicit FBT seem to remain across a wide range of variations to the explicit FBT paradigm. In particular, there are variations of the task which pose a question about the agent's behaviour (e.g. where will Maxi look for the chocolate?) as well as variations which ask directly about the agent's mental state (e.g. where does Maxi think/believe the chocolate is?). The Pragmatic Development Account alleges that children fail the explicit FBT because they systematically misunderstand questions about another person's belief, but if this is the case then they should have less problems with a task, which asks for the prediction of behaviour. However, asking about behaviour rather than belief seems only to have a minor effect on children's performance (Psouni et al., 2018; Wellman et al., 2001). Secondly, while there have been a few variations which do seem to boost performance in line with the predictions from the Pragmatic Development Account (e.g. Hansen, 2010; Rubio-Fernández and Geurts, 2013), these tasks were carried out with 3-year-olds who, it might be argued, were already close to passing the explicit FBT. This differs from the key findings from the implicit FBT, which already show success at the age of 15 months. While there is evidence that modifying the situational context can boost performance somewhat, we currently only have evidence for a limited effect in children already close to the age of passing the explicit FBT. It is also worth bearing in mind that while some studies have shown the effect of situational factors, this effect sometimes only consists in bringing children up to chance level (Kulke and Rakoczy, 2018; Wellman et al., 2001) and performance under these circumstances is fragile (Rubio-Fernández, 2018). This is very different to the robust systematic success in the explicit FBT which we find in the children who are older than 4. This seems to indicate that while situational factors can influence performance somewhat, they do not entirely change the developmental progression and cannot offer a full explanation of the paradox of false belief understanding. A final point to remember is that the 3-year-old children who fail the explicit FBT already are quite linguistically developed and in fact make use of belief terms in conversation (Bartsch and Wellman, 1995). If children were already making use of belief terms, it would seem puzzling if they then fail the FBT because they are unfamiliar with belief discourse and therefore systematically misunderstand the question. This criticism should be treated with some caution, however, because although children do already use belief terms at this stage, there are different uses of belief terms, and it may be that children at this stage predominantly understand belief terms as a means to express uncertainly (i.e. I believe the book is in the drawer, but I am not sure), rather than as an expression of a mental state. Overall, what these criticisms indicate is that although situational factors do play a role in influencing children's performance, some form of cognitive development is also required in order to fully account for the development underlying the paradox of false belief understanding.

Westra is not opposed to this. In fact, he explicitly endorses Carruthers (2013) account on which children fail the explicit FBT because it poses a triple mindreading challenge. However, these two proposals stand separate and are not integrated with each other. The role that executive function might play in Westra's belief discourse focused account is not clear. It is unclear what the role of situational factors – in this case with experience with belief discourse – has on executive function, if any; or what impact the development of executive function skills has on children's appreciation of belief discourse.

3.4 Late Competence Accounts

The evidence that situational factors impact performance seems – at least at first sight – to be more in line with the late competence accounts. If belief understanding is something that has yet to be *learned*, it is easier to see how experience my play an important role. This, however, is true to varying degrees of the different accounts. For example, Apperly and Butterfill's (2009) account does not have a clear role for experience. On their account, the first and second systems are notably independent of each other and the system 1 remains in place alongside system 2 once system 2 has come online. It is therefore at least unclear what role experience has for the maturation of system 2.

Heyes' (2014b, 2018) account falls on the other side of the spectrum in allowing much room for the role of situational factors. Indeed, Heyes' account is special in that she endorses a late competence account and argues that the implicit FBTs do not provide evidence of early belief attribution (Heyes, 2014a) but thinks that the development towards belief understanding does not require a domain specific development, but rather the new combining of domain general 'cognitive gadgets' in new ways. In particular, she also emphasises the role of teaching for the development of mindreading and belief understanding. Because of this, Heyes' account faces some of the same problems as the nativists – namely that the effects of teaching and situational factors are limited. We find improvement predominantly in children who are already fairly close to passing the explicit FBT. For example, Clements and Perner (1994) carried out a teaching study and found that performance was only improved in those groups who already showed signs of belief understanding in their version of the implicit FBT (N.B. these children were 3 years old). This all suggests that there is some internal cognitive development required that could not be fully supplemented by situational factors or even teaching.[5] The picture that emerges is one of a developmental timeline that can be shifted slightly but not suspended entirely.

Perner and Ruffman (2005) agree with Heyes that the performance on the implicit FBT should not be interpreted as evidence of belief attribution. Instead, they argue that simple behaviour rules are sufficient to make sense of infants' performance on the implicit FBT. As with Heyes account, this non-mentalistic reading seems problematic as there are by now a wide variety of implicit FBTs pertaining to show the flexibility of children's competence. While low-level explanations may be possible for individual tasks, it is the variety of implicit FBTs that we have now which lends support to the view that children are sensitive to the perspective of others and attributing beliefs to make sense of their behaviour. The reasoning that children show genuine belief understanding for the explicit FBTs was based on the wide range of explicit FBTs they are able to pass at age 4 (Wellman et al., 2001), and the same reasoning has been applied to the findings from the implicit FBT (Scott, 2017, see also Section 2.2.). Different behavioural rules would be required for the different paradigms, whereas a mentalistic explanation can straightforwardly explain all the findings. Aside from such considerations of parsimony, it is also worth bearing in mind that the set-up of many of the implicit FBTs is very similar to that of the explicit FBTs. What exactly is the difference between implicit and explicit FBTs that allow us to conclude that explicit FBTs require belief attribution while implicit FBTs do not? After all, in the classic Maxi paradigm (H. Wimmer and Perner, 1983), when the child is asked where Maxi will look for her chocolate, the child could also predict this based on behaviour rules. While some researchers have argued that the explicit FBT too does not require belief attribution (Burge, 2018; Povinelli and Vonk, 2003),[6] this is not the view taken by the late competence accounts which we are considering here. On these accounts, the explicit FBT is supposed to detect a genuine development of belief understanding that aims to explain the change in performance.

---

5 In line with Heyes' general account, this cognitive development could be spelled out in terms of a development in the ability to combine domain general abilities in new ways.
6 See Section 1.2.1 for further discussion of these criticisms of the FBT.

While I do not think that we can give a purely behaviourist interpretation of children's performance on the implicit FBTs, I also do not want to claim that these young infants already show a full understanding of beliefs. The implicit FBTs do not require a full reflective understanding of the mental state of belief, nor, for that matter do many of the explicit FBTs asking for behaviour prediction. Undoubtedly there is some development in children's understanding of beliefs that takes place, the question is what the nature of this development is.

I will therefore leave aside the question of whether children's performance in the implicit FBT shows belief attribution, and focus on their account of development. This remains the same, whether this is a development from early belief understanding to a late and more advanced belief understanding, or from behaviour reading to mindreading (specifically belief attribution). Perner (1991) developed an account of belief understanding according to which belief attribution requires being able to meta-represent. On his view, therefore, what develops between children's passing the implicit FBT and their passing the explicit FBT at age 4 is the ability to meta-represent. For our purposes, there are two problems with this account. Firstly, how this meta-representational ability develops is left unclear. Secondly, the role of situational factors in this development is left open – it is both unclear why some situational factors would make meta-representation easier in concrete task context,[7] or why certain experiences would help in the ability to develop meta-representational thinking. This is not to say that such an account of development could not be provided, or that this account is incompatible with situational factors playing such a role. Perhaps meta-representation is something that is learned through experience, but how this would happen is not yet spelled out in the account. These are not fatal criticisms of the account, but rather highlight some open questions that, however, are critical for the purpose of this book, namely providing an account of the development of belief understanding. For this reason, I will leave this account aside for now.

More recently, Perner et al. (2015; Perner and Leahy, 2016) have developed a new approach making use of mental files (building on the ideas of Recanati, 2012). The advantage of mental files is that they provide a useful tool for thinking about cognitive development and are a means of providing a more detailed account of cognitive development. I will be making use of this tool in the next chapter in developing the mental files account. I will therefore leave more detailed exposition of this account to a later stage. As it stands, however, Perner

---

7 Note that Perner and Ruffman (2005) would not accept an extension of the effect of situational factors to make sense of the findings of the implicit FBT. They argue that infants succeed in the implicit FBT because this does not actually test mindreading. I do not think, however, that they would make the same claims about the modified explicit FBTs mentioned in 3.2.

et al.'s mental files account is phrased purely in cognitive terms. The cognitive development is spelled out in terms of changing relations between mental files ('linking') without any mention of how situational factors contribute to this development or performance on the task itself. Given that we have seen that situational factors do play a role in the development of belief understanding, making clear how these fit into the account remains an important open question.

The final late competence account to be considered is the Theory Theory Account developed by Gopink and Wellman (Gopnik, 1993a; Gopnik and Wellman, 1992; Wellman, 1990, 2002, 2014), which might be considered to be the prototypical late competence account with a central role for learning. According to Gopnik and Wellman, children's understanding of the mental states of others depends on their having a theory of these states. Akin to scientists, children are constantly refining and revising their theory in light of new evidence (Gopnik, 1996). At first children only have a theory of mind in terms of desires, with beliefs being a theoretical construct added to the theory later following new evidence and theory revision. While this account does consider the interrelation of situational factors and cognitive development (the situational factors being the evidence required for cognitive development in terms of theory revision), it incurs strong demands in terms of its strong commitment to theory and theory revision as the driving force of cognitive development. Furthermore, the nature of theory formation and revision with the child as a 'scientist' have been left unclear (Gopnik and Wellman, 2012) and have incurred substantial criticism (e. g. Carruthers, 1996). Recently, Gopnik and Wellman (2012) have developed a Bayesian version of their Theory Theory account which aims to address some of these concerns in providing a more detailed account of the theory revision procedure which is also embedded within a highly influential framework in current debates. Overall, while I share Gopnik and Wellman's approach concerning the significance of considering both situational and cognitive factors, the account I will develop in the next chapters differs from theirs in that the cognitive development will be spelled out in terms of mental files and does not share the strong commitment to theory. This does not mean that it could not also be spelled out in terms of the Bayesian framework, but exploring this avenue goes beyond the scope of this book.

3.5 A Problem for the Two-Systems Account?

In the previous chapter, I argued that we can distinguish between three stages in the development of belief understanding. For most of the accounts considered here, this is not a problem. For example, there might be different degrees of situational factors affecting performance, or there might be different stages of cognitive development that give rise to these three stages. For example, perhaps the active helping behaviour paradigm requires some further cognitive development than the looking behaviour paradigm, but not as much as the explicit FBT. This seems plausible when thinking about the early competence accounts where the cognitive development is in the form of increases in executive function. It may be more difficult for late competence accounts such as Gopnik and Wellman's (1992) to account for this intermediate stage, but they too could postulate further stages of theory revision to explain the differences in performance. Although most accounts do not actively address such an intermediate stage, it seems that most could be adapted to account for this stage without significant problems.

There is primarily one type of account which one might think is threatened by the three stage development outlined in the previous chapter, namely the two systems account defended by Apperly and Butterfill (2009). This account has become popular as an explanation of the dichotomy of the implicit and explicit FBT. If there are only two systems, then either we have one system for both types of implicit FBT which, as I have argued, does not do justice to the different tasks; or we have one system for early implicit FBT, and one system for late implicit FBT and the explicit FBT, which does not do justice to the findings of the shift at age 4 in performance.

One possible way of dealing with this is to deny that there is actually a three-stage distinction and argue that the two stages of implicit belief understanding can be collapsed into one. As I discussed in the previous chapter, the evidence is still somewhat uncertain in this regard, and while I think that a three-stage development is the best interpretation of the evidence we have so far, this might change in light of future research.

Even assuming that there is a three-stage distinction, however, need not be too problematic for some versions of the two systems account. As I noted in Chapter 3, independently of the specific distinction I have drawn, there is evidence suggesting that while the explicit FBTs form a coherent and cohesive group, this does not seem to be the case for implicit FBTs which have been shown to correlate only loosely, if at all (Rakoczy, 2017; Grosse-Wiesmann et al., 2017). This seems to suggest that while system 2 forms a single, coherent system, system 1 might actually consist of several parallel processes. This would make sense on the idea that system 1 is domain specific and therefore not very generalisable. The idea that there might be several, highly specific, fast and inflexible processes which underlie performance on the implicit FBT, therefore, is not implausible on a two systems account. Apperly and Butterfill's two systems account could therefore be compatible with three stages of development.

The point at which Apperly and Butterfill's (2009) account differs from that sketched here is that they argue that the two systems are independent from another, whereas I have suggested that we find a continuous development in belief understanding. Contrary to what is suggested by the two-systems account, I do not think that we can draw a sharp distinction between the different stages of belief understanding. Instead, what we find is a gradual increase in the complexity of the tasks that children are able to pass, in keeping with the idea of a gradual development of belief understanding (see Section 2.3).

3.6 Conclusion

In this chapter, I reviewed some of the main accounts in the literature on the paradox of false belief understanding. I focused in particular on the role of cognitive and situational factor in these explanations and argued that previous accounts in the literature usually focus predominantly on one or the other factor, with little attempt to integrate the factors or consider how they might interact across development. This holds true across both early competence and late competence accounts. In this chapter, I argued that such a focus is problematic, leaving the accounts unable to account for some of the empirical findings. We require an account that considers both cognitive and situational factors in conjunction in order to provide an empirically adequate account of the FBT.

This is not to say that accounts in the literature with a predominant focus on only one factor are incompatible with – or do not allow for – a role of the second factor. Indeed, most accounts do – at least in principle – allow that both cognitive and situational factors impact on development. Nonetheless, there is an important story to be told about how the two factors interrelate across development that has so far not been adequately addressed. This will be my task in the next chapter.

4 Situational Mental File Account

In Chapter 2 I discussed the different kinds of FBT and argued that there are three developmental stages underlying the paradox of false belief understanding. My aim in this chapter will be to develop a new Situational Mental File Account of the paradox of false belief understanding.[1] This account builds on the work of Joseph Perner et al. (2015; Perner and Leahy, 2016) who have recently argued for mental files as a "useful tool for cognitive development… [which] capture[s] important aspects of cognition" (Perner and Leahy, 2016, 491). Mental files provide the benefit of allowing a more detailed exploration of the nature of cognitive development underlying differences in performance. As noted in the previous chapter, one of the problems with cognitive development accounts is that the nature of the cognitive development is often left unspecified or at least underspecified. Using the mental files framework can help with this.

While I agree with Perner et al. (2015; Perner and Leahy, 2016) in their use of mental files as a model of cognitive development, I will expand and modify the account to provide an explanation of the three stage developmental trajectory outlined in Chapter 2. I do this by integrating situational factors into Perner et al.'s purely cognitive account. One of the core tenets of my account is that cognitive and situational factors are intricately interwoven in development. We must therefore consider both factors and how they interact in development.

First, I introduce the central features of mental files (Section 4.1.) and how Perner et al. apply this to the FBT (Section 4.2.) which I then develop into the new Situational Mental File Account (Section 4.3.).

4.1 Mental Files

I begin by introducing the central features of the mental files framework. There are two key features of mental files: the files themselves and the linking relations between them. I will introduce these two in turn in this section. Mental files store information on objects. In short, they are "tool[s] for managing information about an object in the world" (Perner et al., 2015, 78). A mental file for an object contains the information on the object. For example, the mental file for my pen would contain information like, "has blue ink" and, "is made of metal".

---

1 The Situational Mental File Account was first introduced in Newen and Wolf (2020). This chapter is based on and elaborates some of the ideas introduced in this co-authored paper.

https://doi.org/10.1515/9783110758610-008

Mental files are based on 'acquaintance relations' (Lewis, 1999; Recanati, 2012), i.e. the means by which we gain information on the object. For instance, I can gain information about the physical features of an object through seeing the object, i.e. a perceptual acquaintance relation. For example, when I see the pen I can add information about its physical appearance to my file. There are, however, many ways of gaining such information. I can also gain information about an object through someone telling me about it, for example if I have not used the pen myself yet but have merely been told that it has blue ink. The function of the mental file is to bundle all the information I have on an object such that the information is not only stored, but that this information is systematically integrated and interconnected.

Importantly, in the case of a mental file of an individual object, which we are related to by direct reference, the reference of the mental file is the anchoring relation.[2] Perner and Leahy (2016) describe this in terms of "anchoring": the file is anchored in the real-world object. This means that if the pen actually has black ink, my mental file still refers to that silver pen lying on my table, even if the information in the file does not fit the real-world object. This means that misrepresentation based on false information does not lead to failed reference (Recanati, 2012). The anchoring of the mental file in the object is shown in Figure 4.1.

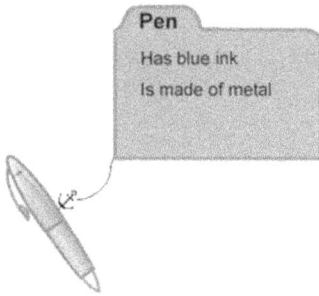

Figure 4.1: Mental file of the pen containing information and a label, anchored in the real-world object. Figure modified from Newen and Wolf (2020, *Figure 1, 729)*

2 This relation need not be epistemically transparent. A well-known example of this is the case of Hesperus and Phosphorous. For the ancient Greeks these were the names for the evening star and the morning star respectively, both of which refer to Venus (i.e. they have the same reference). However, it was not known at the time that these terms both referred to the same thing. There are also some circumstances where mental files might be individuated by the content of the file, for example when we only have a descriptive concept, e.g. "The murderer of Smith whoever it was" (Newen, 2010) without knowing who this refers to.

This distinction between the anchoring of the file – its reference – and the information stored in the file – its sense – is of great importance in philosophy of language. I will not delve into these issues here, but see Recanati (2012) for an extended discussion of mental files as applied to problems in philosophy of language. Important for our purpose is that more than one mental file can be anchored in the same object. Suppose, for example, that the pen was a Christmas present from my grandmother. In this case, I can have two mental files that are both anchored in my pen: 'pen' file shown above, along with the file for "my Christmas present". These files may be separate, especially if I have forgotten what the gift from my grandmother is. Nonetheless, both of these files refer to the same object, namely the pen, but they may contain different information. For example, my 'Christmas present' file may contain information that my grandmother gifted it to me, that it was wrapped in red paper and so on. Perner et al. (2015) argue that every time an object is introduced with a new label – where labels are individuating information such as "pen" or "Christmas present" – a new file is created.[3]

Mental files are informationally encapsulated. As Recanati (2012, 43) puts it: "informational integration and inferential exploitation of information only takes place within files, on this picture". This means that only information within the file is available for reasoning. For example, when thinking about my pen as 'pen' I can conclude that it will write in blue, but the information that it was a present from my grandmother is not available to me.

This encapsulation is highly problematic, as we often need to reason about the information contained in more than one file, for example when thinking about co-referential files with different labels. The solution is the linking of files as "when two files are linked, information can flow freely from one file to another, so informational integration and exploitation [across files] becomes possible". (Recanati, 2012, 43). It is this linking between files that would allow me to conclude that my grandmother gave me a pen with blue ink for Christmas (Figure 4.2.).

There are a number of contexts in which linking is important. In the example considered above, there is linking between co-referential files, i.e. files that refer to one and the same object. This is the form of linking which I will focus on in this chapter. It is worth bearing in mind, however, that linking of files is likely to

---

3 We should be cautious about taking this claim too strictly. It would be rather inefficient if we had to create a new mental file every time we learned a new label for an object. However, in most circumstances a new label is a good indication that a new object is being picked out. Therefore, the rule that when we encounter a new label we create a new file may be best thought of as a good heuristic that children also use.

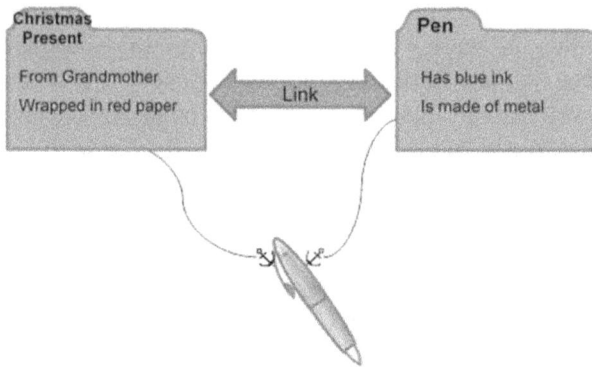

Figure 4.2: Two co-referential mental files anchored in one object. Both files are linked allowing for the flow of information between files.

be a very prevalent phenomenon that is used in many different contexts. For example, if I store the information that the pen "is on the table", this might involve a link to my 'table' file.[4] Similarly, Recanati (2012) also suggests that recognising a particular object as an instantiation of a general concept is a case of linking files. For example, recognising this pen as a *pen* requires linking the 'pen' file from working memory with the 'pen' file from long-term memory. It is an open question whether we really need to widen the notion of 'linking' to account for all these cases, but I want to stay neutral concerning this debate. While there can be many different types of linking between mental files, it is the ability to link two co-referential and previously unconnected files which is of central importance to the discussion of the FBT. Similarly, I also allow that there can be mental files for different entities (for example: persons, situations, events[5]), but for the purposes of the following discussion I will focus on mental files of individual objects and the dynamics of linking between such co-referential mental files.

In many cases, the linking between co-referential files can be present from the start. I usually know that the pen was a gift from my grandmother. In this case, the 'pen' file was created when I opened the gift from my grandmother and hence was linked from the start with my 'Christmas present' file. However, this is not always the case, as shown by the famous Hesperus and Phosphorus

---

4 See also (Perner and Brandl, 2005) for a similar idea in terms of discourse referents.
5 See Hommel (2004) for arguments why we need event files for understanding object cognition.

example. Both refer to the planet Venus, but this was not known for many years. It was only once this was discovered that both files could be linked, allowing the flow of information. To give a different example, I spent some time searching for papers written by Wendy Clements after the year 2000, failing to realise that she was now publishing under her married name Wendy Garnham and that therefore, the paper that I was searching for was one which I had in fact already read. Putting this in terms of mental files, I had two mental files – one 'Wendy Clements' file and one 'Wendy Garnham' file, both of which were anchored in the same person. As the files were unlinked, there was no flow of information between the files. It was only once I realised that Wendy Garnham was her married name and that the two therefore refer to the same developmental psychologist that I was able to link the files and therefore access the information about her more recent papers.

4.2 Mental Files and the False Belief Task

Perner et al. (2015; Perner and Leahy, 2016) apply the mental files framework to the FBT. In order to do so, they postulate *vicarious mental files*, which were originally suggested by Recanati (2012) as a way of representing the mental states of others. Vicarious mental files are like *regular mental files* in that they have labels and content, but they are *indexed* to another person. What this means is that this mental file corresponds to the mental file in the mind of another person.[6] These files are also anchored in the object. For example, suppose that I know that my pen actually has black ink, but Francis, who has only read the packaging, thinks that the pen has blue ink. In this case, I have a regular mental file for the pen with the information that the pen has black ink. I also have a vicarious mental file also anchored to the same pen indexed to Francis, which contains the information that the pen has blue ink. This vicarious mental file allows me to track Francis' beliefs about the pen (Figure 4.3).

Applying this to the classic FBT, where Maxi's chocolate has been moved from the green box to the blue box without Maxi's knowledge, there are two mental files for the object: firstly, the regular mental file which represents the chocolate as being in the blue box, and the vicarious mental file which represents the object as being in the green box. This vicarious mental file is indexed to Maxi, meaning that it is to be understood as "Maxi's Chocolate File" (Perner

---

6 Or rather, the mental file that the other person is supposed to have. One may, of course, be mistaken about the beliefs of another person.

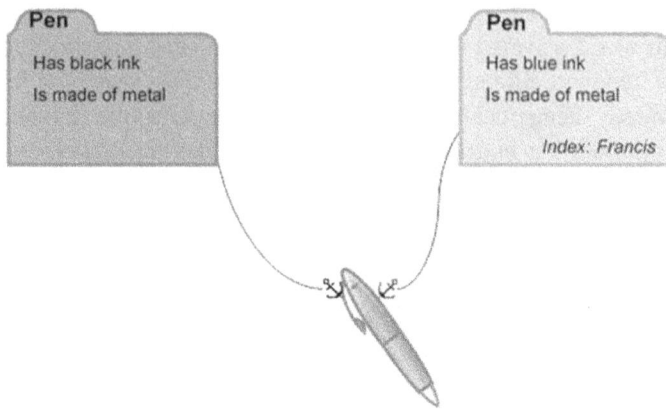

Figure 4.3: Co-referential vicarious and regular mental file. Vicarious mental file of the pen indexed to Francis. Both the vicarious and the regular mental file are anchored in the same object.

and Leahy, 2016). Both files are co-referential and anchored in the same object, but they contain different information about the object.

In order for information to be accessed across files, they must be linked. This means that for unlinked mental files only the information stored in one of the files is available at a time. Concerning this linking Recanati (2012) distinguishes between horizontal linking – which is the linking that takes place between two regular mental files – and vertical linking – which is the linking between regular and vicarious mental files. While the horizontal linking in the case of co-referential regular mental files signifies a strong identity relation and allows for the free flow of information between files,[7] vertical linking between a regular and a vicarious mental file only allows for restricted information access. For example, when linking the files "Wendy Clements" and "Wendy Garnham" the informa-

---

7 While Recanati (2012) speaks in terms of flow of information, in this Chapter I will follow Perner and Leahy (2016) in thinking about the linking relation more in terms of accessing information. While there may be flow of information sometimes when linking regular mental files (horizontal linking), when thinking about representing different perspectives we do not want the information from the vicarious mental file to be moved to the regular mental file. The information in the vicarious mental file should not be mixed with the information in the regular mental file unless I am updating my own beliefs about reality based on the information from someone else. Nonetheless linking should allow the information in the vicarious mental file to be accessible. Whether horizontal linking usually involves a flow of information or is also something best thought of in terms of information access is something I leave open here.

tion about the papers she has authored can move freely between the files. In the case of vicarious mental files, however, such a free flow of information would be problematic, as I need to be able to track someone else's perspective without this information then changing my own perspective – especially in the context of false beliefs. Perner et al. (2015; Perner and Leahy, 2016) argue that till the age of 4 children are unable to link mental files.[8] This means that they are only able to access the information stored in the regular mental file and not the vicarious mental file. This leads them to give the wrong answer in the explicit FBT (Figures 4.4 and 4.5).

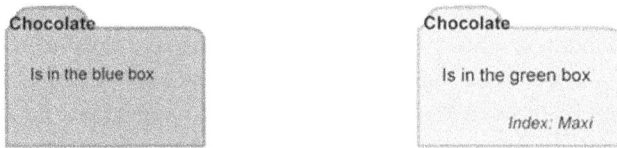

Figure 4.4: Unlinked mental files in the FBT. Children have two mental files in the FBT: a vicarious mental file (indexed to Maxi) and a regular mental file that are initially unlinked. The anchoring relation is left out of the following figures for the purposes of simplicity. Figure modified from Newen and Wolf (2020, Figure 4a, 732).

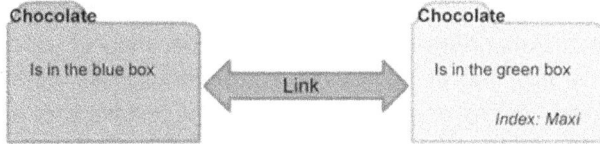

Figure 4.5: Linked mental files in the FBT. Children only pass the FBT when they are able to link mental files at age 4. Figure modified from Newen and Wolf (2020, Figure 4b, 732).

There are a number of reasons why the mental files framework is useful for providing an account of the development underlying the paradox of false belief understanding. Firstly, the mental files framework allows for a detailed explora-

---

8 Note that Perner et al. are only talking about the linking (both horizontal and vertical) between co-referential files and not linking of the form "the \<pen\> is on the \<table\>", which may be achieved independently. Similarly, if there is linking required in order to recognise something as an instantiation of a particular, or recognising that this is the same object over time as suggested by Recanati (2012), this may also be a different independent form of linking which occurs between different systems of memory. I do not think that Perner et al.'s account of the development of linking underlying the FBT – nor mine for that matter – commits us to any claims about these other forms of linking.

tion of the cognitive development taking place. As we saw in the previous chapter, the lack of a clear account of the nature of cognitive development was a problem, especially for some of the late competence accounts.

Secondly, although the mental files framework derives from the work of Recanati (2012), who makes use of mental files in order to address issues in philosophy of language, there are also precedents for making use of something similar to mental files in psychology, namely object files (e.g. Kahneman et al., 1992). These featured in the literature on children's ability to track objects. The idea of using 'files' as a means of modelling cognition is therefore not foreign to psychology. As Murez and Smortchkova (2014) note, however, mental files and object files are not the same. In particular, mental files of the kind that Recanati (2012) uses to address issues in philosophy of language depend on long-term memory, while object files were thought to be a means of tracking objects in working memory. The core of Murez and Smortchkova's argument, however, is that object files are insufficient to do the heavy lifting that Recanati requires in order to address the relevant debates in philosophy of language. This is not important for my argument, as I am interested in modelling cognitive development and not mounting an argument in favour of descriptivism in philosophy of language. Given the nature of the FBT, the mental files used would be held in working memory anyway. Therefore, the distinction between mental files and object files is unproblematic for our purposes and can be left aside. Furthermore, Recanati (2012) himself describes different types of mental files, some of which are from long-term memory and concern our general concepts of objects but also some others which are generated upon (e.g. perceptual) acquaintance with an object and which would be held in a working memory 'buffer'. What is missing, therefore, is a detailed account of how these different mental files relate to each other. A full account of this, however, would require an extended discussion of the literature on different memory systems and how these relate to each other, such that mental files can be retrieved from long-term memory and held in working memory. This, however, goes far beyond an understanding of the processes underlying the FBT and exceeds the scope of this chapter.[9]

Thirdly, one advantage of this explanation of children's failure in the explicit FBT is that it makes sense of the correlation between children's performance on

---

9 The only place where this might be relevant is concerning the "smarties task", which is an unexpected contents FBT. This task depends on children having some background knowledge about smarties boxes and their contents, which may need to be retrieved from long-term memory. However, in this task the key ability being tested is not children's ability to recognise a smarties box and remember the contents. Therefore, while memory retrieval may be required in some forms of the FBT, this is not the central dimension of the task.

the explicit FBT and other 'perspective changing' tasks such as the alternative naming task (Doherty and Perner, 1998; Perner et al., 2002). In this task, children are asked to play a game where they must provide an alternative name for an object. For example, they are shown a stuffed rabbit and told that this can be called either a rabbit or a bunny. If the experimenter says rabbit, they must say bunny and vice versa. Till the age of 4, children are very bad at this task, usually repeating what the experimenter said. At the same time, however, they do not have the same problems if the task is to report the alternative colour of a blue and green teddy: if the experimenter says "green" children *do* say "blue". Perner et al. (2015) interpret both the failure in the explicit FBT and the alternative naming tasks as the result of an inability to link co-referential files. In the alternative naming task, children have two files for the object: one under the label of "rabbit" and one under the label of "bunny", both anchored in the same object. As the children under 4 are unable to link mental files, when the experimenter says "rabbit", the children are only able to access the 'rabbit' file and not the 'bunny' file. Therefore, they too say "rabbit", thereby failing the task. Similarly, in the explicit FBT, in the absence of linking children only have access to the information stored in their regular mental file. Therefore, when asked where Maxi will look for her chocolate they respond that he will look in the blue box, as this is where the chocolate is represented as being in the regular mental file, hence failing the task.

Finally, the mental files framework has already been used to generate novel and interesting predictions (Perner and Leahy, 2016) which have partially been tested and confirmed (Huemer et al., 2018). While the use of mental files in this area of research is still very new, this indicates that the mental files framework is a useful tool for thinking about cognition as it has already generated promising testable predictions.

There remain, however, a number of open questions concerning the mental files account. Firstly, the role of situational factors is left unclear in this account. Perner, Rendl and Garnham (2007) only briefly mention that bilinguals may have an advantage in perspective shifting tasks because they are confronted with 'alternative naming tasks" all the time in virtue of speaking two languages, but the nature of how these situational factors interrelate with the development of the linking ability is left largely unclear. Secondly, Perner et al.'s account does not provide an explanation of children's success on implicit FBT paradigms. This means that, as it stands, it does not provide an explanation to the paradox of false belief understanding. Thirdly, it is unclear how the ability to link mental files develops. A final open question is the nature of the vicarious mental file and how this relates to the regular mental file.

My task, here, will therefore be to elaborate on the mental files framework in the form of a Situational Mental File Account. This extends the framework to also cover the findings from the implicit FBT. I argue that situational factors play an important role at this early stage and are crucial to setting up the linking between mental files. I will also provide a more detailed account of the nature of the linking relation and the vicarious mental files. The vicarious mental file will be the topic for the next chapter.

One open question that I will not be addressing here is the question whether and how the mental files framework might be implemented neurally. For our purpose here, the mental files framework is being treated as a computational level framework that aims to provide an account of how children's belief understanding develops. How this might be implemented in the brain is a further matter. Nonetheless, there is also some recent brain imagine evidence which provides tentative support for the mental files framework as they found overlapping areas of brain activation for various tasks which require linking of mental files i.e. tasks which require considering different perspectives (Arora et al., 2015). While this is promising for the mental files framework as it suggests that there may be neural correlates of something like a 'linking process', more research is required in order to establish a proper account of the implementation.

4.3 The Situational Mental File Account

In order to provide an explanation of the performance in the implicit and the explicit FBT we must consider how the different mental files are activated. I suggest two principles of activation (Newen & Wolf, 2020, 731– 732):

1. *Situational Factors Principle.* If a person has two mental files of an object, namely a regular and a vicarious mental file, then which file is activated depends on situational factors. If the situational factors trigger a focus on the object, the regular mental file is activated. If situational factors trigger a focus on the other person, then the vicarious mental file is activated.[10]

2. *Cognitive Factors Principle.* If a person has two mental files of one object, namely a regular and a vicarious mental file, *and there is a linking relation between the files*, then if one of the files is activated (through situational factors), information from all files accessible through the link is available.

---

10 Similarly, if there are two regular mental files for an object (as is the case in the alternative naming task), which of these files is activated may also be determined by situational factors shifting the focus such that one file is activated or the other.

This means that prior to linking, only situational factors determine which information is available in virtue of determining which file is activated. Once linking is achieved between files, the most adequate information for the task can be *selected* from all the files, which are accessible through the link. I will begin by commenting on each of the two principles before using them in order to model the three stages of development of belief understanding identified in Chapter 2.

4.3.1 Situational Factors Principle

Fundamentally, the Situational Factors Principle rests on the idea that situational factors can highlight certain aspects of a test situation. There is considerable evidence that situational factors can have an effect on cognitive processes and performance. For example, priming studies have shown that attention can be modulated by the context in which stimuli are presented and aid object recognition (Chun, 2000). Similarly, there is evidence that contextual priming has an effect on the language comprehension of ambiguous words: if the word 'bank' is mentioned in a financial context, I am likely to interpret this word as referring to the financial institution. If, however, I am discussing rivers, I interpret 'bank' as referring to the river bank (Gennari et al., 2007). In terms of mental files, this can be interpreted as situational factors (i.e. the context in which the stimuli are presented) facilitating the activation of a mental file (over another). This means that situational factors influence what is *salient* for us and therefore which mental file is activated. While the notion of salience is complex, all I mean by salience here is that situational factors can change the weighting of certain features. Without claiming to provide a detailed account of the mechanisms underlying this, I suggest that this would include bottom-up and top-down attentional mechanisms. Wellman et al. (2001) similarly make use of the notion of salience to refer to task modifications that serve to highlight the perspective of the other person as opposed to reality.

Applying this to the FBT, this means that if situational factors determine which mental file is initially activated, then factors, which highlight the other person's perspective, should facilitate performance in the FBT.[11] There is some evidence for such a facilitating effect of situational factors. One well known study which investigated the role of aspects of the task setup on performance

---

11 Similarly, if the situational factors highlight the object and not the other person's perspective, this should impede performance on the FBT.

is that of Rubio-Fernández and Geurts (2013), who modified a variety of features of the classic FBT in the attempt to boost performance. They argued that the reason why children typically fail in the explicit FBT is that the task is set up in such a way that it disrupts children's perspective tracking. They identified two important modifications that were jointly able to boost performance: Firstly, the child was frequently reminded of the other person's perspective throughout the experiment.[12] Secondly, rather than asking the child the classic question of, "Where will Maxi look for the chocolate?" the question was instead changed to, "What happens next?" The reasoning for this is that the question, "Where will Maxi look for the marble?" places a focus on the object and its actual location and thereby disrupts children's ability to track the other person's perspective (Rubio-Fernández, 2013). These findings can be expressed in terms of mental files: reference to the chocolate highlights the object, which causes activation of the regular mental file rather than the vicarious mental file. This means that children only have access to the information of where the chocolate actually is from the regular mental file. The perspectival information contained in the vicarious mental file is not accessible.[13] The findings from this study fit well with the account being developed here: if the situational factors such as the task set-up are modified such as to introduce or maintain a focus on the other person, then children's performance in the FBT improves.

There is also further evidence that modification of the FBT set-up, which introduces a stronger focus on the perspective of the other person, can improve performance. For example, Lewis et al. (2012) conducted a study in which they tested children's understanding of beliefs and found that children's performance

---

12 This also involved a modification where the agent (in this case a Duplo doll) was moved such that she could not observe the change in location, but did not leave the scene entirely. Rubio-Fernandez and Guerts speculated that having the agent leave the scene might also disrupt perspective tracking. Given that we have evidence of children succeeding in implicit FBTs where the agent did leave the scene (e. g. Buttelmann et al. 2009), it seems that with the appropriate situational cueing children might be able to return to the perspective.

13 Attempts to replicate the findings from Rubio-Fernández and Geurts (2013) have struggled to fully replicate the original findings, with some only replicating the findings in older children (Kulke and Rakoczy, 2018). In one such replication study, Kammermeier and Paulus (2018) found that although children were better at the Duplo Task than the standard FBT for both ages 3 and 4, the performance of 3-year-olds in both the Duplo task and the standard FBT did not differ from chance. Only at 4-years-old were children above chance at the Duplo Task. This limited replication fits with the view proposed here that situational factors can impact children's scores on the task, but that cognitive development is necessary for the development of false belief understanding too, and seems to constrain the effects of situational factors, i.e. there was some improvement, but not sufficient for performance to be boosted above chance in the 3-year-olds.

improved if another person was added to the false belief scenario who also observed the change in location. That is to say, that children were more accurate in determining the beliefs of the other person in a scenario in which there were two seekers looking for a hidden object as opposed to one. On first sight, these results seem puzzling: by adding another person it would seem that there is an extra person whose perspective needs to be taken into account, which would appear to make the task more demanding as there is more information to be processed. However, what adding the other person may do is highlight the different perspectives in the situation and their relevance to the task. This means that although the situation now seems more complex, the setup is such that the perspective of the other person is highlighted. This increases the chances of the vicarious mental file being activated, leading to an overall improvement in performance. Evidence in the same direction is provided by a study by Hansen (2010), who showed that asking, "You and I both know where the chocolate is, but where will Maxi look for the chocolate?" improved children's performance in the FBT. Interpreting this study is not unproblematic, as the question may have been overly suggestive and biased children towards the correct response. Nonetheless, this evidence is in line with the general idea being developed here, namely that if the task is set up so as to emphasise the perspective of the other person, then access to the vicarious mental file containing information on other people's beliefs is facilitated. A different way of highlighting perspective is in the form of a memory aid, as done by Mitchell and Lacohée (1991). They used a version of the smarties task in which children were required to post a picture of what they initially thought was inside the box. Only then were they shown what was really in the smarties box. This posting modification was found to improve performance, with the majority of children passing the task. Mitchell and Lacohée interpret this as the memory aid serving to highlight and preserve the child's own past perspective.

Highlighting due to situational factors should always be thought of as relative, with vicarious and regular mental file competing for activation. Therefore, the vicarious mental file can be activated either by highlighting the perspective of the other person as in the examples above, or by reducing the salience of reality, for example if the children themselves do not know the real location of the object or the object is removed from the scene. There are several experiments showing that children's performance on the explicit FBT improves if the object in question is removed from the scene entirely (Mascaro and Morin, 2015; Mascaro et al., 2017; Wellman and Bartsch, 1988). Reducing the salience of reality – and hence reducing the propensity towards activating the regular mental file – facilitates the activation of the vicarious mental file.

The evidence considered so far has been based on the explicit FBT and modifications thereof, which have improved performance.[14] The same reasoning, however, can be extended to the implicit FBT. In the implicit FBT focus on the other person is either sustained (e.g. Onishi and Baillargeon, 2005) or the return of the agent places a focus on the other person (Buttelmann et al., 2009). This leads to the activation of the vicarious mental file, allowing children to access the perspectival information and therefore pass the task. This is unlike the explicit FBT where, as mentioned above, the question, "Where will Maxi look for her chocolate?" places an emphasis on the object (Rubio-Fernández, 2013; Rubio-Fernández and Geurts, 2013). This focus on the object leads to an activation of the regular mental file containing the information of where the object actually is, not the vicarious mental file. If mental files are unlinked – as we hypothesise is the case in children under the age of 4 – then only the information in the file activated is accessible. This means that if the question introduces a focus on the object and therefore activates the regular mental file, then children will only be able to access the information from the regular mental file. The information from the vicarious mental file is not accessible and therefore children will fail the task. This indicates that the problem in passing the explicit FBT lies not in being able to represent another person's perspective, but rather in being able to access this information. When files are unlinked, this access is dependent on whether the relevant file is triggered through situational factors and children are unable to access this information in a systematic situation-independent manner.

4.3.2 Cognitive Factors Principle

The Cognitive Factors Principle is based on the ideas of Perner and Leahy (2016) who argue that children develop the ability to link mental files at the age of 4. At this point, the information accessible to the child does not only depend on which mental file is activated due to situational factors. The linking relation therefore signifies the achievement of a degree of detachment from the immediate situation and should be understood as increasing the cognitive flexibility of the child. It is this ability to link mental files, which allows children to pass the explicit FBT at age 4.

---

14 Although the Duplo Task by Rubio-Fernández and Geurts (2013) has sometimes been considered as an implicit FBT (Kulke and Rakoczy, 2018).

Going beyond the work of Perner et al. (2015; Perner and Leahy, 2016) I want to suggest that there is not only full bi-directional linking, but that there can also be uni-directional linking – i. e. information from file A is accessible from file B, but information from file B is not accessible from file A (see also Newen and Wolf, 2020). What I mean by this is that prior to the development of the ability to fully link mental files at age 4 children may already be able to establish a link from the vicarious mental file to the regular mental file but not vice versa.

Intuitively it seems plausible that it is easier to establish a link from vicarious to regular mental file than vice-versa and that therefore linking may not always be fully reciprocal. As adults, when thinking of someone else's perspective we clearly remain aware of our own view on the matter, and our own perspective may even automatically suggest itself (especially if the other person's perspective differs from ours). It is not usually the case that when thinking about another person's perspective we forget our own view on the matter or confuse the other person's view with our own. This indicates that we remain aware of our own perspective when thinking about the perspective of the other person. Remembering to take into account someone else's perspective when thinking about my own perspective requires more effort (Bradford et al., 2015). A common example of this can occur in conversations on a topic where we have much expertise and may use jargon without realising that the other person is unaware of what they mean. This difference in the linking may in part be due to our own perspective being the default or more salient in some way, although I will later also suggest that there may be cases of uni-directional linking which do not involve the distinction between our own perspective and that of another person (see Chapter 5).

In what follows I will argue that postulating such a uni-directional link as an intermediate stage allows us to account for the active helping behaviour, which I have argued in Chapter 2 should be seen as a distinct developmental stage. Moreover, via this uni-directional link it is possible to tell a developmentally plausible story of how the linking between mental files comes to be set up, which I will do in Section 4.3.4.

4.3.3 Interaction between Situational and Cognitive Factors

One of the open questions of Perner et al.'s mental files account is, how is the linking relation initially established? In order to provide an answer to this, we must consider the interaction between situational and cognitive factors. So far, I have outlined how situational factors can facilitate performance in the task itself. However, we also know that situational factors can have a long-term effect on performance. For example children whose parents make use of more mental state talk perform better in the explicit FBT (Ruffman et al., 2002, see also Section 3.2.). This can be understood as an indirect effect of situational factors; that is to say, that situational factors not only directly influence performance in the task itself, but that they also trigger cognitive development which, in turn, leads to an improved performance on the FBT. As I will show in more detail below, the active helping behaviour paradigm provides a good example to see how an initial link between mental files gets set up. In this helping behaviour task the vicarious mental file is initially activated through situational factors (direct influence). In order to help, however, the child must act on reality and it is this situational activation of the vicarious mental file, combined with the need to act on reality that allows for an initial link between the vicarious and regular mental file to be set up (indirect influence). Similarly, while maternal mental state talk or having an older sibling do not impact on the task itself, they play a role in increasing a child's sensitivity to perspective. Both provide opportunities for the situational highlighting of other people's perspectives, which over time leads to an increased sensitivity to other people's perspectives. This increased sensitivity then facilitates cognitive development in the form of linking. Putting this in terms of mental files, the highlighting of other perspectives – be it though the mother's discourse, or by being confronted with another's perspective when one has a sibling – leads to an activation of the vicarious mental file and might even facilitate being able to construct vicarious mental files (direct influence). This leads in turn to a cognitive development facilitating the retrieval of the vicarious mental file in other situations too (indirect influence).

The interrelation between cognitive and situational factors goes in both directions (see Figure 4.6. for an overview of the interrelation between cognitive and situational factors in the development of belief understanding). Situational factors not only lead to cognitive development, but cognitive development can also lead to a greater sensitivity to situational factors. This can simply be in terms of being able to handle greater information loads, which allows for a greater sensitivity to situational factors. If the child is not overwhelmed by the demands of the task, it is more likely that they will be able to pick up on the situational cues to guide them which information is relevant to the task in question. Going beyond this, however, it is likely that cognitive development, in particular in terms of an increasing discourse understanding, improves children's understanding of a situation, imbuing them with a greater sensitivity to situational cues. This point is related to Westra's (2016) idea that children fail the explicit FBT because they lack experience with belief discourse and thereby fail to realise that the question they are being asked concerns the mental states of the other person. Unlike Westra, however, I do not want to limit this merely to the understanding of the question, but also include other factors such as cultural practices or other non-linguistic cues in the setting of a task that indicate that the perspective of the other person will be important for the task. Cognitive development not only increases children's sensitivity to a greater number of situational factors, but also allows for a better weighting of these factors in order to determine what is relevant for the task. Furthermore, being able to link mental files and therefore relate different perspectives to reality may help with determining the relevance of perspectival information in a given situation.

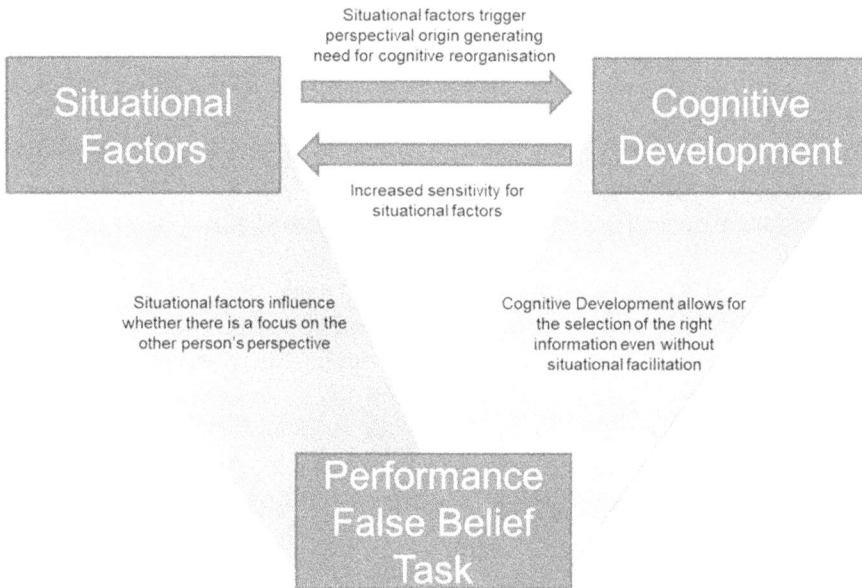

Situational factors trigger
perspectival origin generating
need for cognitive reorganisation

Situational
Factors

Cognitive
Development

Increased sensitivity for
situational factors

Situational factors influence
whether there is a focus on the
other person's perspective

Cognitive Development allows for
the selection of the right
information even without
situational facilitation

Performance
False Belief
Task

Figure 4.6: The interrelation between cognitive and situational factors for performance in the FBT. A combination of situational and cognitive factors determine performance on the FBT. Cognitive and situational factors are inter-dependant: cognitive development may increase sensitivity for situational factors, and situational factors play a role in shaping cognitive development.

This shows that there is a substantial co-dependence between situational and cognitive factors. A central claim of the view being developed is that situational and cognitive factors do not just impact false belief understanding independently, but that these factors interact in important and interesting ways.

4.3.4 Three Stages of Development

Following the introduction of the mental files framework and the discussion of the principles of activation of mental files, I will now use this in order to provide a new account of the paradox of false belief understanding. In other words, using the mental files framework in order to map out both cognitive development and the role of situational factors, I will provide an account of the three-stage development from implicit to explicit FBT (first outlined in Chapter 2).[15]

Stage 1

This stage is exemplified by many of the classic implicit looking behaviour based FBTs such as those by Onishi and Baillargeon (2005) or Southgate et al. (2007) which children already pass at the age of 15 months, with some evidence suggesting even earlier success (Kovács et al., 2010). At this stage, the child is only required to take the perspective of another person without having to relate this to their own.

In terms of mental files, this stage is characterised by unlinked mental files (Figure 4.4). Children are unable to link mental files and therefore which information they have available is entirely determined by situational factors, as these decide which mental file is activated. If the situation emphasises the other person, this primes the activation of the vicarious mental file. This vicarious mental file contains the perspectival information, i.e. the information on the object from the perspective of the other person. This information is all that is required in order to pass this type of task, as the child is not required to make use of their own knowledge concerning the object. This means that if situational factors activate the vicarious mental file, they are able to access the perspectival information they need and are able to pass the task. If, however, the task is such that the situational factors highlight the object, the regular mental file is activated and the perspectival information is not accessible, leading children to fail the task.

This is not to say that there is no role at all played by cognitive mechanisms like inhibition. Even though the task may highlight the perspective of the other person, it is still the case that the child has a different perspective on the situation, which may still need to be inhibited to some extent. Therefore, some basic inhibition abilities may be required in conjunction with the situationally facilitat-

---

15 See also Newen & Wolf (2020).

ed activation of the vicarious mental file. This level of inhibition, however, falls far short of a linking between mental files.

Stage 2

This stage is exemplified by the active helping behaviour task that children pass at 18 months. Passing this type of task requires some linking between perspectives as the child must determine the experimenter's goal based on the experimenter's (mistaken) perspective, while acting to 'help' the experimenter requires the child's own perspective.

In terms of mental files, this stage still starts with the activation of the vicarious mental file due to situational factors. For example, in the original Buttelmann et al. (2009) study the experimenter returns and tries to open the box. This places an emphasis on the experimenter leading to the activation of the vicarious mental file. This vicarious mental file contains the perspectival information needed in order for the child to determine the experimenter's goal, i.e. the desire to retrieve the toy. In order to help the experimenter, however, the child requires the information where the toy actually is, that is to say information contained within the regular mental file. As the child can only help by acting in reference to reality, the child reverts back to the regular mental file (containing the information where the toy actually is) in order to help the experimenter. This means that the need to act on reality leads to the activation of the regular mental file, and therefore allows for an initial systematic transition from vicarious to regular mental file. This call for action may itself be considered a situational factor, which leads to a shift from vicarious to regular mental file. The difference to the early situational facilitation, which is also found in stage 1, however, is that the information from the vicarious mental file concerning the goal of the other person remains available throughout the shift. In other words, while using the vicarious mental file to determine the goal of the other person, the child is able to access the information from the regular mental file on where the object actually is. This means that there is a *uni-directional* link from the vicarious mental file to the regular mental file: following the activation of the vicarious mental file due to situational factors, the information from the regular mental file is also accessible (Figure 4.7). It is important to note, however, that at this point in the developmental story there is no link yet from the regular mental file to the vicarious mental file. This means that the vicarious mental file is only accessible following in virtue of activation by situational factors. As I will show below, this allows us to explain why young children who pass the active helping behaviour task nonetheless fail the explicit FBT.

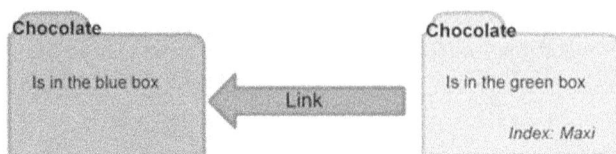

Figure 4.7: Uni-directional linking from vicarious to regular mental file. There is a link from the vicarious mental file – representing Maxi's perspective of the chocolate as being in the green box – to the regular mental file, which represents the child's own knowledge of the situation. Figure modified from Newen and Wolf (2020, Figure 5, 373).

An experiment which provides further evidence that there is at least a uni-directional link from the vicarious mental file to the regular mental file is from Mascaro and Morin's (2015). In this experiment, 3-year-olds were able to infer the location of an object after being told of another person's belief about the location of the object and that this belief was mistaken. In this scenario, given that children did not know the actual location of the object and that the belief of the other person is discussed, the focus is on the other person's perspective and hence the vicarious mental file is activated. From this, however, children were then able to draw conclusions about reality. This example differs slightly from the one given above in that children did not need to draw on information in their regular mental file in order to pass the task, but rather add information to their regular mental file based on the information they had in their vicarious mental file. Both cases, however, are the same in that they both require a link from the vicarious mental file to the regular mental file. This, however, does not provide any evidence of the reverse link from the regular mental file to the vicarious mental file.

This uni-directional linking requires being able to coordinate more than one mental file. For this reason, executive processes going beyond the basic inhibition of Stage 1 are required. For example, the goal of the other person (derived from the vicarious mental file) must be held in memory when switching to the regular mental file.

One caveat concerning the developmental picture developed above is that in Chapter 2 (Section 2.3.), I discussed the possibility that the distinction between children's early success in the implicit looking behaviour studies and their later success in the active helping behaviour tasks might not hold up. The evidence concerning this, especially in the light of the replication crisis, is open to change, and further research might show that the same level of belief understanding underlies both. Although this would significantly change the picture of development, combining these stages would not be fatal for the account that I am developing, as the central claim that we need a stage of uni-directional linking remains. The only difference would be that this uni-directional linking stage would underlie both the early looking behaviour based studies as well as the active helping behaviour studies. While the looking behaviour tasks do not require being able to link different perspectives, it could be that children are in fact already able to uni-directionally link mental files in the same way as required by the active helping behaviour. One point to note about this, however, is that the looking behaviour studies *on their own* do not provide positive evidence for the uni-directional linking ability, as this is not required to pass the task. We only get positive evidence for such a uni-directional linking when children pass the active helping paradigms that do require children to link different perspectives.

Stage 3

Stage 3 is characterised by full belief understanding as evidenced by the explicit FBT. As in stage 2, the explicit FBT requires the child to coordinate both the vicarious and the regular mental file. The direction of coordination here, however, is in the reverse direction, namely from the regular mental file to the vicarious mental file. Therefore, the uni-directional link from vicarious to regular mental file is insufficient, as children also need to be capable of a link from regular to vicarious mental file. This means that full linking is required at this stage (Figure 4.5). The reason for this is that the question posed places the focus on the object (as discussed in Section 4.3.1). This activates the regular mental file, therefore making necessary a switch from the regular mental file to the vicarious mental file in order to access the perspectival information.

Unlike in the active helping behaviour task, it is unclear whether this need to switch between perspectives is an inherent part of the classic explicit FBT. As in the looking behaviour based implicit FBTs, in order to pass the task, the child only needs to draw on the information from the vicarious mental file. The information from the regular mental file is not needed at all and can be disregarded. Children's early failure in the explicit FBT where they show a consistent reality bias, however, indicates that their regular mental file is activated and that a switch is necessary. There are ways in which the specific set up of the task prime the regular mental file, for example by referring to the name of the object (Rubio-Fernandez and Geurts, 2013). As we saw above, if these aspects of the task are removed, children's performance improves. A further possibility is that language may play a role. While we saw that language also features in other types of FBT, the explicit FBT specifically has the experimenter pose a direct question to the child. Importantly, the experimenter posing the question usually shares the child's perspective and this too may highlight the child's own perspective at the cost of the diverging perspective of the other agent

(Helming et al. 2016). Furthermore, an underlying cooperation bias as postulated by Helming et al. may lead the child to systematically misinterpret the question as being about the actual location of the object rather than the belief. This would lead to the initial activation of the regular mental file, hence making a link to the vicarious mental file necessary in order to access the information within this file.

There is also some support for this from a study by Rubio-Fernández (2013). Using eye tracking, she provided evidence that a disruption in belief tracking also occurs in adults when being asked the classic explicit FBT question. While their looking behaviour indicates that they are initially tracking the perspective of the other person, when asked a question like, "Where will Maxi look for her chocolate?", they look towards the actual location of the object, which is interpreted as a shift from the perspective tracking to the actual object. Although adults therefore show a similar disruption in perspective tracking, they are able to recover from this while children are not. The hypothesis here is that it is due to adults' ability to link mental files that they are able to recover from the distraction. Children (below the age of 4) without the ability to link mental files or who only have a uni-directional link from vicarious to regular mental file are not able to recover and return to the vicarious mental file. In the absence of a link from regular to vicarious mental file, children are dependent on situational factors for the activation of the vicarious mental file and therefore cannot recover from such distraction.

How can such a link from regular to vicarious mental file be achieved? There are two components that may contribute to this development that I want to highlight here. Firstly, the pre-existing uni-directional link may play an important role as it begins to connect mental files that may facilitate access to the vicarious mental file at a later stage. Secondly, developments in language acquisition may play an important role in furthering the linking ability. Through language, the format of mental files or their organisation may change allowing for more flexible access to information. While there are proposals arguing for such a role of language for the development of belief understanding (for example, Berio, 2020; de Villiers and de Villiers, 2014), how this might be integrated within a mental files framework remains an open question.

The linking of mental files leads to some independence from the immediate situational factors and allows children to succeed even in the absence of situational facilitation. As with the previous stages, this bi-directional linking comes with a number of increasingly sophisticated executive processes. These include things like the deliberate selection of the relevant information: if linking allows for more flexible switching between files, more information from different files is available and the correct information in the context of the task must be selected. For example, in the explicit FBT, the relevant perspectival information from the vicarious mental file must be selected in order to pass the task. It is important to note, however, that even at this stage situational factors still play an important role in determining which mental file is activated. For many everyday situations, this initial situationally driven activation of files may be sufficient. The important difference when being able to link mental files is, however, that one is not limited only to the file that is situationally activated. Furthermore, it is important to remember that this decoupling from the situation that is achieved through the linking of mental files is itself a development that arises out of the early successes due to situational factors. It is situational factors, which initially trigger the perspective of the other person and thereby generate the need to relate the perspective to reality for action. The initial systematic link is generated through the early situationally facilitated sensitivity to the perspective of another person, which is then used to adjust one's own behaviour. Therefore, although the ability to link mental files allows for a level of decoupling from the situation, situational factors play an important role in shaping the development of the decoupling itself.

4.3.5 Belief Understanding

What does the linking relation consist of? This question is particularly important in the context of the debate discussed in Chapter 3 between empiricists and nativists. Does the development merely consist in an increase in executive function of working memory, or does it signify a genuine change in children's understanding of beliefs. It is clear that working memory and executive function play an important role for the linking of mental files. This is especially important given that this means that there is *more information available* for the child, which must be *selected*. Both working memory and executive functions such as inhibition mechanisms clearly must play an important role in this. However, is this all there is to the development of linking mental files? In Chapter 3, I reviewed some reasons for being sceptical that the development of false belief understanding consists purely in developments in working memory and executive function, which I will not rehearse again here. At the very least, situational factors must play an important role in how to *use* these increased working memory abilities and executive function skills.[16] I want to go further, however, and argue that a certain

---

[16] This would be similar to the view of Westra (2016) who argues that while children have an early belief understanding, they must yet learn how to employ this correctly in conversation. A key difference to my view – even on this more constrained view of cognitive development

level of working memory and executive function abilities is not only needed for the *use* of belief understanding, but that these abilities are necessary for an understanding of belief itself. In order to understand beliefs, one must at least have an understanding of perspective, specifically that there can be *more than one view of one and the same thing* (Perner et al., 2002).[17] This means that one must not only be able to take different perspectives on one and the same thing, but one must be able to put them together and relate them to each other. In other words, to have an understanding of beliefs, one must be able to construct more than one perspective, and these perspectives must be related to each other in a particular way such that the child understands that these different perspectives correspond to one and the same thing. Being able to combine and reconcile different perspectives requires a level of working memory and executive function, which is constitutive of belief understanding and not merely an additional demand, which is specific to the FBT. This does not mean that there are not versions of the FBT, which pose further demands in addition to those required by belief attribution. But this does mean that even if we consider the development of the linking ability to be purely an increase in terms of working memory and executive function, this is still a significant change in the child's mental organisation, where this increase in executive function abilities is still constitutive of a development of belief understanding.

One objection to my claim that understanding belief requires a certain level of working memory and executive function would be to say that children have an innate theoretical understanding of belief, which they are perhaps unable to exercise properly till working memory and executive function are sufficiently developed. In other words, children could have an understanding of belief but not be able to exercise this till they have a certain age.[18] However, this argument only works if we think of understanding belief in terms of having a *concept* of belief, where some views of what it means to have a concept allow for having a concept which one is not able to use correctly yet. On this view, a concept might be

---

– is that situational factors affect not only the understanding of the question and learning when beliefs are relevant in discourse, but underlies the linking of files themselves.

17 A similar argument has recently been made by Phillips and Norby (2019) who argue that being able to attribute beliefs to others requires being able to keep this perspective distinct from one's own.

18 Although there are some nativists who credit children with an innate concept of mind (e.g. Leslie, 1987, 1994, Leslie et al., 2005) I do not take this to be their view. They argue that children are able to use their understanding of mind in contexts other than the FBT. It is the FBT itself, which poses too high demands on the child, not that children have a concept of belief but are incapable of engaging in belief reasoning because of additional demands.

thought of as a piece of mental machinery that the child either has or does not have, even if they cannot yet put it to proper use given limitations in executive function. As I have noted at the beginning of this book, however, I am interested in belief understanding as an *ability*. Therefore, it is the question of how and when children are able to exercise this ability and the development of this ability that interests me here, rather than whether children have some innate piece of mental machinery.

What does this mean for the findings from the looking behaviour based implicit FBT (Stage 1)? While at this stage there is no full linking between files and therefore no genuine belief understanding, there is still an early sensitivity to perspective, which is the basis of a later belief understanding. This sensitivity to the perspective of the other person is still an important component of our social understanding, even if it falls short of belief understanding. Things are more difficult concerning the uni-directional linking stage (Stage 2). Here children are able to relate perspectives to each other to some extent, but the ability to access the perspective of the other person is still limited to situational factors. On the one hand, authors such as Phillips and Norby (2019) argue that the ability to consider two distinct perspectives simultaneously and keep them distinct as shown in the active helping behaviour paradigms should be sufficient for belief understanding. On the other hand, Perner and Leahy (2016) maintain that the full linking at age 4 signifies belief understanding. While the uni-directional linking does provide evidence of an early ability to relate different perspectives, it must be remembered that this is still fragile and strongly dependent on situational facilitation. It is only available under particular circumstances, as children are still unable to activate the vicarious mental file independently of situational cueing. Whether this should already be classed as belief understanding depends on how robust this uni-directional linking is, and whether we can find it across a variety of different contexts. Currently, the evidence in this regard is still limited. Regardless of the question whether Stage 2 should already be classed as belief understanding, the level of understanding in Stage 3 is clearly a different one and marks an important step in the development of belief understanding. It is much more robust and evidences a level of insight into the relation of different beliefs and perspectives, which allows for access to the other's perspective even in the absence of situational facilitation.

4.4 Conclusion

In this chapter I argued for the Situational Mental File Account as an empirically adequate account of the paradox of false belief understanding, arguing for a three-stage development from unlinked mental files, via uni-directionally linked mental files to fully linked mental files. Situational and cognitive factors interact throughout this development, with early performance being largely determined by situational factors. Cognitive development, which is shaped by situational factors, allows for some degree of situational independence, but situational factors remain important.

There are a number of advantages of this account. Firstly, making use of the mental files framework we are able to provide a clearer account of the nature of cognitive development underlying the paradox that, as we saw in Chapter 3, was a critical point for accounts looking at the cognitive development underlying the development of mindreading. Secondly, the Situational Mental File Account considers both the role of cognitive and situational factors and how these inter-relate across development. While initially mental files are unlinked and therefore situational factors largely determine which mental file is activated, the cognitive development of linking mental files allows for some detaching from the immediate situational context. Furthermore, situational factors play an important role for the cognitive development as they provide the original situational triggering for the development of linking between files. Thirdly, the Situational Mental File Account provides a new explanation of the paradox that specifically accounts for the intermediate helping behaviour stage in terms of uni-directional linking.

While I have argued for the Situational Mental File Account as a promising account of the paradox of false belief understanding, further investigation into the role of situational factors and how this relates to cognitive development would be beneficial. The Situational Mental File Account has the benefit of making testable predictions concerning the role of cognitive and situational factors (Newen and Wolf, 2020). A key prediction is that children – especially before they are able to link mental files – will do better in a task that places an emphasis on the other person than in a task that places an emphasis on the object. If the task emphasises the other person, this facilitates the activation of the vicarious mental file and allows children to pass the task. If the task emphasises the object, the regular mental file will be activated, causing children to fail the task. If the account is correct that children perform better on implicit FBTs *because* these place an emphasis on the perspective of the other person, then modifying the task to place an increased focus on the object should lead to a drop in performance. One way of doing this might be to have a toy, which is very attractive to the child (e.g. a favourite toy) or an item, which is attention grabbing (e.g. a ball with flashing lights). This should remain true, even if the task remains indirect and non-verbal. Similarly, varying who the person is whose perspective must be tracked could also impact performance. The account would predict that if the person in question is someone who is important or interesting to the child (e.g. a parent), this would introduce a focus on the person and facilitate activation of the vicarious mental file, leading to an improvement in performance.

A further area where situational factors may play a role in triggering the vicarious mental file is in false belief tasks involving deception, where the active involvement of the child in generating a false belief in another person may serve to highlight the perspective of the other person. The evidence concerning children's understanding and ability to make use of deception are mixed (consider, for example, Reddy and Morris (2004) and Wellman et al. (2001)). Further consideration concerning whether the intention to deceive is sufficient to highlight the other persons perspective, or an active engagement in the deception is required would be needed to tease apart these results. Doing so here would go beyond the scope of this book, however, I will return to this issue in Chapter 6 when considering the closely related phenomenon of pretend play.

Similarly, an area that remains to be investigated is the role of testimony within mental state attribution. Intuitively it would seem plausible that if the other person voiced their false belief, this should trigger a perspectival representation and activate a vicarious mental file, improving children's performance on the false belief task. A study on this was conducted by Riggs and Robinson (1995), who had a 'message condition' in which the agent first voiced their false belief, before the child was asked what the agent's belief was. Riggs and Robinson found no benefit for children who heard the message as opposed to children who did not hear the message. However, it is unclear whether children were able to maintain focus on the vicarious mental file, or if their regular file was activated when being asked about the agent's belief (as suggested by the work of Rubio-Fernández (2013), see also Section 4.3.4). Therefore, further research in this area is required in order to test how testimony influences children's mental state attribution and what role this plays in the interaction between cognitive and situational factors.

This account is based strongly on the notion of vicarious mental files that is used to represent the perspective of the other person. In the next chapter I will focus on some of the open questions concerning the nature of vicarious mental files, especially how and when they are created.

5 Finding a Point of View: Vicarious Mental Files and Perspective Taking

In the previous chapter, I outlined the development of social understanding in terms of mental files, indicating how the initial linking between mental files is set up in development. There, I assumed that there can be unlinked vicarious mental files and that this allows us to explain the findings from the implicit FBT paradigms. This assumption, however, is controversial. Perner made use of such unlinked vicarious mental files in his early papers (e.g. (Perner and Brandl, 2005) and has suggested that such unlinked files can be used to provide an explanation for early successes in implicit FBT paradigms (Doherty and Perner, 2020; Perner, 2016). In contrast, in some other recent papers he asserts that "without it [the ability to link mental files] children cannot form the vicarious mental files necessary to capture another person's false belief" (Perner and Leahy, 2016, 502). Similarly, Recanati (2012) claims that vicarious mental files must always be linked to their corresponding regular mental file. My assumption that there can be unlinked mental files therefore requires some defending, which I aim to offer in this chapter.

As discussed in the previous chapter, regular mental files are based on acquaintance relations: a new file is created every time we encounter a new object. How does this work concerning vicarious mental files? There are two questions to be asked here: firstly, *when* are vicarious mental files created and, secondly, *how* are they created. I will mainly be concerned with the latter of the two questions, but briefly comment on the former question (Section 5.1.). I then consider the most prominent argument why one might think that vicarious mental files must be linked to regular mental files and show that this argument fails to establish this, also providing some arguments in favour of unlinked mental files (Section 5.2.). In doing so, I will draw specifically on evidence from the literature on visual perspective taking (Section 5.3.).

5.1 When Do We Create Vicarious Mental Files?

When do we create vicarious mental files? There are two main possibilities to answer this question. First, vicarious mental files could be created every time we encounter another person, so we create a mental file for every object the person

https://doi.org/10.1515/9783110758610-009

has an epistemic relation to.[1] The second possibility is that we create vicarious mental files only to the extent that the other person's perspective diverges from our own, with the regular mental file performing a dual role till an incompatibility is reached. This would mean that per default, information is shared and it is only when there is a divergence that different perspectives come to be represented. The difference between both accounts can be illustrated using the example of the Maxi FBT (Wimmer and Perner, 1983) where Maxi places his chocolate in the cupboard and then leaves the room. On the first account, a vicarious mental file is created for Maxi right from the start when Maxi first appears to place his chocolate. On the second account, the vicarious mental file would only be created when Maxi leaves and the chocolate is moved, leading to a difference in the perspectives on the chocolate.

Both views have some merits to them and the evidence is currently inconclusive. In favour of the former is that perspective taking seems to happen automatically, regardless of whether the task requires this or not (Elekes et al., 2016; Samson et al, 2010).[2] This could be interpreted that we automatically create a vicarious mental file whenever we encounter another person. However, evidence in favour of automatic perspective taking is usually based on tasks where there are diverging perspectives, so it could also be argued that we only automatically create vicarious mental files *when perspectives diverge*. Indeed, the evidence that subjects take longer to respond in conditions of diverging rather than of shared perspective could be taken to suggest that vicarious mental files are only created under conditions of diverging perspectives, where the cognitive effort in producing and maintaining the further mental file leads to the delay (Samson et al., 2010). However, it could also be argued that the time delay is not due to the creation of the vicarious mental file, but from the extra computation, which is required in order to determine the content of the vicarious mental file. The evidence from perspective taking therefore seems insufficient to conclusively support the view that vicarious mental files are generated automati-

---

1 For the sake of simplicity, I will only consider mental files of objects here, where objects are taken to be things in the world.

2 There is some evidence that automatic perspective taking is limited (Surtees et al., 2016). So, for example, that we only compute whether someone has seen something and not how this is seen (Apperly and Butterfill, 2009). This would suggest that if we do create vicarious mental files automatically these are limited and would require further, non-automatic elaboration if needed. This limitation does not concern, however, whether the perspective of the other person is shared or not. Therefore, the limitations of automatic perspective taking do not indicate that vicarious mental files are not automatically created whenever we encounter another person. All it shows is that, if vicarious mental files are created automatically in this way, then these files are subject to some limitations.

cally whenever I encounter another person, regardless of whether perspectives diverge or not.

In favour of the latter view – that we create vicarious mental files only when there are diverging perspectives – is that this would be a more parsimonious mental file management system with fewer superfluous mental files. Especially if we think that updating and maintaining mental files comes with some cognitive effort, it would be good not to unnecessarily inflate the number of mental files one is dealing with. Furthermore, the 'Curse of Knowledge Bias' (Birch and Bloom, 2007; Camerer et al., 1989) – i.e. the bias to overattribute our own perspective and assume that others know what we know – might be counted as evidence in favour of this view. If we only create vicarious mental files when a perspective differs from our own, we may sometimes fail to take note of the divergence and therefore mistakenly continue to use our regular mental file. However, the over attribution of our own perspective can also be explained on the view that we create a vicarious mental file every time we encounter another person. On this view, the overattribution error is due to a mistake in mental file management, such as mistakenly copying too much information from our own mental file when creating the vicarious mental file.

Huemer et al. (2018) have recently done some work pertaining to how information from the regular mental file is used in creating a vicarious mental file. They showed that 4- to 6-year-old children who are capable of linking files and pass the FBT tended to mistakenly copy links from their own regular mental file (with other files) to the vicarious mental file. To test this, they made use of an ambiguous object that looked like a dice but was actually an eraser and varied whether children knew about the actual identity of the object before or after encountering another person. For example, if the child knew that the dice was actually an eraser, they mistakenly attributed this knowledge to the other person as well, even though the other person was not privy to the demonstration of identity. The important finding was that children's error depended on whether they encountered the other person before they were shown the identity of the object, or after. If they encountered the other person before the identity was revealed they did not make the mistake – at this point, their own regular mental files were unlinked, so the unlinked file of the dice was copied to a vicarious mental file. If, however, they encountered the other person after the identity claim was revealed, children copied the linked regular mental file of the dice (linked to the eraser file) as a vicarious mental file for the other person.

This finding is interesting and tells us something about how vicarious mental files are created and managed, but I do not think that this study is able to tell us anything about the question of *when* a vicarious mental file is created as both accounts would be able to explain these findings. The task is aimed at testing whether the time at which we encounter another person influences information transferred from the regular mental file, rather than whether the encountering of another person is sufficient for the creation of a vicarious mental file.

While I am tentatively in favour of the view that the vicarious mental file is created when perspectives diverge (i. e. when there is incompatible information), I think the evidence in this area is currently not decisive. Both positions would be compatible with the account, which I develop in the remainder of the chapter of how vicarious mental files are created.

5.2 How Are Vicarious Mental Files Created?

I now turn to the second question and consider how vicarious mental files are created. I am especially interested in the question of whether vicarious mental files must be linked to regular mental files or not. I therefore distinguish between two types of view one might have. On the first view, which I call the *Linking Account*, vicarious mental files are created through being linked to regular mental files. This is the kind of view advocated by Perner and Leahy (2016) when they claim that it is the ability to link files which allows children to create vicarious mental files. Recanati (2012) similarly claims that there cannot be unlinked vicarious mental files. On the second *Unlinked Account*, which is the view I will be arguing for, vicarious mental files need not depend on a link to a regular mental file. This means that we can have unlinked vicarious mental files, and that children could have vicarious mental files before they are able to link mental files. While the Linking Account is currently popular in the literature, there have also been some people who have supported the Unlinked Account. For example, Recanati (2012) attributes this view to Perner in his early work on discourse referents (Perner and Brandl, 2005). Similarly, Doherty and Perner (2020) discuss this as a possible explanation of the findings from the implicit FBT.

There are two points of clarification in order. Firstly, in arguing for *unlinked* vicarious mental files, I am not committed to the view that there can be vicarious mental files that do not have a corresponding regular mental file, only that there can be vicarious mental files which are not linked to a regular mental file. It may be that there are cases where there are vicarious mental files without corresponding regular mental files (for example, Perner et al. (2015) give the example where the other person mistakenly thinks that there are two objects in the box while you know that there is only one – here you have one mental file and two vicarious mental files), but there is nothing about the Unlinked Account itself which would necessitate assuming that there are such cases. Furthermore, the Unlinked Account need not assume that in ordinary cases vicarious mental files are not linked to regular mental files. It may be that in most ordinary cases for adults who are capable of linking files, vicarious mental files are linked to regular mental files. All that is needed for the Unlinked Account is that it is *possible* for there to be vicarious mental files, which are not linked to regular mental files. How frequently this takes place is a further question. Secondly, the Linking Account does not have to be committed to the view that every vicarious mental file must be linked to a *corresponding* regular mental file, i.e. they are not committed to their needing to be a one-to-one relation between regular and vicarious mental files. In the example discussed above from Perner et al. (2015) there is no corresponding mental file for one of the vicarious mental files. Nonetheless, this does not speak against the Linking Account as both vicarious mental files may still be linked to the one regular mental file and necessarily depend on that link.

Why do Perner and Leahy (2016) as well as Recanati (2012) think that there can only be linked vicarious mental files? Unlinked vicarious mental files cannot be taken as evidence of a full perspective understanding (see Section 4.3.5), but this alone is no reason for thinking that they cannot exist. It should also be noted that neither Perner and Leahy nor Recanati give any reason why vicarious mental files must be linked to regular mental files. Nonetheless, I do acknowledge that the Linking Account has some intuitive appeal. This, I think, derives from the thought which we find in much of the work on mental files that the contents of the vicarious mental file are *copied* from the regular mental file (Perner et al., 2015). The argument then would look something like the following:

1. Vicarious mental files are copied from regular mental files
2. This copying means that there is a flow of information from one file to the other
3. Flow of information from one file to the other requires linking[3]

Therefore:

4. Copying files requires linking
5. The creation of vicarious mental files requires linking

I will give two responses to this argument. First, I will argue that it is not clear that vicarious mental files must always be copied from regular mental files. Sec-

---

3 In Chapter 4 I said that I would understand linking in terms of information access rather than flow of information. The linking underlying the creation of a vicarious mental file may be special in this regard, because the information accessed actually is transferred to the vicarious mental file. This means that there would be a flow of information here, even if linking need not always involve a flow of information.

ond, I will argue that even if files are created via copying, this does not mean that they are linked in the way required for passing the FBT.

While vicarious mental files may be created through copying some of the time, I do not think that this is the only way in which vicarious mental files can be created. To see this, remember that mental files are supposed to be based on acquaintance relations (Section 4.1.) One way in which this may happen for vicarious mental files is through copying – acquaintance relations of the vicarious mental file are then indirect through the acquaintance relations of the regular mental file. But this is only one way. Another way would be via tracking the acquaintance relations of the other person directly, this means automatically tracking what the other person has seen, for example.[4] This means that rather than copying the information from one's own regular mental file, what the other person sees (or to put things widely is epistemically related to) would be tracked directly in the vicarious mental file independently of one's own perspective. Note that some amount of tracking acquaintance relations independently from the own regular mental file would be required in order to pass any FBT anyway, because what is required in these tasks is that the contents of the vicarious mental file *diverges* from the regular mental file, so mere copying would be insufficient.

Leaving aside the question of whether there can be vicarious mental files without copying, does copying really mean that vicarious mental files must be linked? I will argue that it does not – or rather that the kind of linking which underlies copying is only a *temporary information connection* and is different to that which underlies the linking in the FBT described in the previous chapter. Copying information from the regular mental file to the vicarious mental file does involve a flow of information from one file to another (in this case from the regular mental file to the vicarious mental file) which in a minimal sense is a form of linking. However, there are different kinds of links between mental files. For example, Recanati (2012) distinguishes between horizontal linking, which is between regular mental files of the same order, and vertical linking which is the kind of linking which takes place between regular and vicarious mental files (as discussed in Section 4.2., see also Recanati (2012, Chapter 15, especially p 155) for more details). However, there might be further ways of linking

---

4 This could be akin to tracking 'encounterings' as envisaged by Butterfill and Apperly (2013) for their minimal mindreading account, where an encountering is a relation between an individual and an object within their visuospatial field. Butterfill and Apperly argue that representing such encounterings is limited which might mean that the ability to create unlinked vicarious mental files is limited. This is not a problem, however, for the Unlinked Account, as long as it is possible to have some unlinked vicarious mental files.

files. In particular, the linking that is required for copying information from regular to vicarious mental file need not be such that the link must be maintained once the information has been copied. One suggestion that I am sympathetic to is that there might be an initial temporary information connection allowing for the copying of information from the regular mental file to the vicarious mental file, but that this link is not sustained. In particular, I think one plausible explanation of this is that young children are unable to maintain a link between co-referential files with differing information. On this view, it could be the case that creating vicarious mental files does initially require some form of temporary linking, but that this linking is not sustained resulting in unlinked mental files. This temporary information connection is different from the more robust form of linking achieved at age 4, which can be sustained over differences in content.

Having argued that we can have a story of how vicarious mental files are created without being (or remaining) linked to a regular mental file, I will now give some positive arguments for thinking that there can be unlinked mental files.

The first reason, that has already been noted, is that postulating unlinked mental files gives us the explanatory benefit of being able to account for the findings from the FBT. If children are unable to create vicarious mental files before they are able to link files at age 4, then the early success on implicit versions of the FBT would have to be explained in terms of low-level association processes which, I argued in Chapter 3 (Section 3.4.), are insufficient.[5] It would be good, however, to have some independent arguments in favour of this, especially given the controversy over the findings of the implicit FBT (Dörrenberg et al., 2018; Kammermeier and Paulus, 2018; Kulke and Rakoczy, 2018; Kulke et al., 2017, 2018; Poulin-Dubois et al., 2018; see Section 2.3.3 for discussion).

A second reason for postulating unlinked vicarious mental files comes from the analogy with the alternative naming task. Perner and Leahy (2016) partially motivate their mental files account by arguing that there is a correlation between the alternative naming task and the FBT which can be explained in terms of mental files: both tasks require being able to reconcile different perspectives,

---

5 In Chapter 2 and 4, I also considered the possibility that stage 1 and stage 2 in the developmental sketch might collapse into one stage, this is because although the looking behaviour based FBT does not *require* linking, it could still be the case that even at this stage, children already have this ability. This would leave the heart of the proposal that there is an early stage of uni-directional linking intact. I do not think, however, that this would solve the problem for someone who claims that vicarious mental files only arise out of the link with the vicarious mental file. This is because the creation of the mental file requires a link from the regular mental file to the vicarious mental file, and this is precisely what children lack till age 4, even on the view that there is an earlier uni-directional linking.

that is to say both tasks require the linking of files. In the alternative naming task, it is clear that children already have two existing files. For example, if they are asked to alternate between "dog" and "puppy", both are terms, which they are familiar with and know what they refer to. It is simply the switching between the two, which causes them problems. If we want to draw a close analogy to the FBT, therefore, we should also assume that there are two pre-existing mental files that are only linked at age 4.

This clearly is not a knock down argument against the view that the vicarious mental file is only set up through the linking. It could be, for example, that once one is able to link mental files the creating of vicarious mental files comes 'for free'. It seems, however, that generating a new vicarious mental file should be a computationally demanding process, which should require some more effort than simply linking files without needing to generate a new vicarious mental file in the process. Generating a new file through linking seems to be a more extensive cognitive reorganisation than merely linking two pre-existing files. I would therefore expect that if children are only able to create vicarious mental files through linking, then a task requiring vicarious mental files should be more difficult than a task, which can make use of two already pre-existing mental files. Given, however, that the alternative naming and the FBT seem to be of equal difficulty to children, I think this provides some tentative evidence in favour of the view that there can be vicarious mental files prior to linking.[6]

Finally, as I will consider below, there is evidence from the literature on perspective taking which suggests that children are able to represent another perspective before they are able to relate it to their own. This could be explained in terms of being able to create vicarious mental files without being able to link them to regular mental files. As I will show, we can fruitfully apply the mental files model developed to the previous chapter to explain the perspective taking literature. This supports the idea that there are unlinked mental files and al-

---

6 Considering cases of autism might be useful to look more closely at the relation between linking files and vicarious mental files. If people with autism are able to pass the alternative naming task while failing the FBT, this might indicate linking without the ability to create vicarious mental files. However, this research has currently not been done, although there is some research on the similar ability to reverse ambiguous figures in people with autism with mixed results (Sobel et al., 2005). So further experiments are required in order to test this idea. Furthermore, the later passing of explicit FBT's by people with autism who are able to engage in linking could suggest that people with autism are only able to create vicarious mental files to linking, which leaves open the possibility that normally developing children may be able to create vicarious mental files earlier in a different manner. The matter of autism is very complicated, however, and risks conflating many factors, so any conclusions reached because of this are tentative at best.

lows us to further deepen our understanding of vicarious mental files and how they come about.

5.3 Perspective Taking and Perspective Contrasting

In the literature on perspective taking, we find the important distinction between level-1 perspective taking and level-2 perspective taking (Flavell, 1988). While level-1 perspective taking requires only understanding that different people may see different things, level-2 perspective taking requires understanding that different people can see the same thing in different ways. In other words, level-2 perspective taking requires a sensitivity to the fact that the same object can be seen in different ways. While children master level-1 perspective taking already at 14 months (Sodian et al., 2007), children typically do not pass tasks requiring level-2 perspective taking till the age of 4 (Flavell et al., 1981). My focus in this section will be on the level-2 perspective taking task, which bears close similarity to the FBT.

The fact that children pass the FBT and level-2 perspective taking tasks is no coincidence. Both tasks correlate (Flavell, 1988). Both tasks place similar demands on the child as both require understanding that there can be different ways of conceiving of one and the same thing (Perner et al. 2002). There are also differences, however. The FBT, like the alternative naming task is an example of conceptual perspective taking while the level-2 perspective taking task is a test of visual perspective taking, with the former requiring the child to consider different ways of conceiving of one object, while the latter requires considering different visual perspectives on one object. The level-2 perspective taking task, like the FBT, usually requires interpersonal perspective taking (although there can be variants of both task which require taking one's own past perspective). This is different to the alternative naming task, where there is less of an interpersonal element. Despite these differences, the tasks still correlate well with each other and children pass them at around the same time, suggesting that there is something specific about perspective taking *in general* which is mastered at this point (Perner et al., 2002).

Here it is necessary to introduce some key terminology in order to understand what exactly is meant when talking about perspective taking. As mentioned above, in the literature we find the distinction between level-1 and level-2 perspective taking. Within level-2 perspective taking we can also distinguish between perspective taking and perspective contrasting (Moll et al., 2013). Perspective taking only requires being able to determine the perspective of the other people without having to relate this to one's own perspective or reality. Perspective contrasting requires being able to link or relate perspectives to each other, i. e. understanding that the different perspectives one is able to take are actually different perspectives on one and the same object. Perspective contrasting is needed for an understanding of perspective. These differences are shown in Table 5.1.

Table 5.1. Different levels of Perspective Taking

Level-1	Perspective taking	A sensitivity to whether someone has access to an object or not
Level-2	Perspective taking	Generating alternative perspectives on an object
	Perspective contrasting	Linking different perspectives of an object

Returning to the transition in performance that we find at age 4 in perspective taking tasks, what is it about perspective taking which is mastered at this point? Is it the ability to generate alternative perspectives (i. e. perspective taking), or is it the ability to link different perspectives (perspective contrasting)? There is evidence from the perspective taking literature in favour of the latter. In a series of experiments Moll et al. (2012, 2013) have shown that 3-year-old children are already capable of level-2 perspective taking, provided their own perspective is not emphasised. In one experiment (Moll et al., 2013), the child and the experimenter were sat on opposite sides of a table with a screen made half of yellow glass and half of transparent glass after having been allowed to walk around and familiarise themselves with the apparatus. Two blue objects were then placed before the yellow glass and the transparent glass on the side of the child such that the child saw two blue toys while the experimenter saw a blue toy and a green toy (due to the yellow glass). When the child was asked by the experimenter to pass the green toy, the children were successful in picking out the toy in front of the yellow screen. Therefore, even though both toys looked blue to them, they seemed to understand that the one in front of the yellow screen would look green to the experimenter. If, however, the experiment was modified such that the child's own perspective was highlighted, children failed at the task. For example, if they were asked to indicate (based on a colour sample) what *that toy* looks like to them and what it looks like for the other they were unable to complete the task. Moll et al. interpret this as evidence that 3-year-olds are capable of 'perspective taking' but not of 'perspective contrasting'.[7] In other

---

7 In the other experiment testing perspective contrasting, Moll and Tomasello (2012) showed that if children were given two objects, one of which was a chocolate and one of which merely

words, they are able to generate different perspectives, but are unable to link them. This coheres well with the picture I have been developing with mental files, namely that children are able to create vicarious mental files early on, but only develop the ability to link these files at the age of 4. This means that if their own perspective is highlighted they will be unable to access the information from the vicarious mental file, hence failing the task.

There is, however, some criticism to be made of this task, Moll et al.'s (2013) perspective taking and perspective contrasting conditions are quite different so it could be that the difference in performance between the two conditions was due to other factors than the perspective taking/perspective contrasting difference. For example, in the perspective taking condition children simply needed to pass one of the toys to the experimenter, while in the perspective contrasting condition children were asked a more complicated linguistic question ("What does it look like for you?", "What does it look like for her?") and indicate this on a separate colour sample. The perspective contrasting condition, aside from the difference in perspective taking/contrasting, appears to be an easier and more direct task. It could therefore be that children merely performed poorly in the perspective contrasting condition because they did not understand the question they were being asked, or were confused by the samples they were supposed to point at.

While it would be good to have a repeat of the experiment with better matched conditions, I do not think that these methodological questions fully undermine the data. The key insight from Moll et al.'s study is that there was a condition in which children were able to succeed in the perspective taking task. In contrast, we have not only their perspective contrasting condition, but a significant literature using a range of level-2 perspective taking tasks in which perspective contrasting is required showing that children do not succeed (Flavell, 1992; Flavell et al., 1981). Given this, the claim that children are able to pass Moll et al.'s tasks, while failing the standard level perspective taking tasks because they are capable of perspective taking but not perspective contrasting remains a good explanation. The studies by Moll et al. therefore provide further evidence that there can be unlinked vicarious mental files and that there is a de-

---

looked like a chocolate but was actually an eraser, children were able to tell which one was really the chocolate and which one merely looked like a chocolate. When they were only shown the ambiguous object that looked like a chocolate but was actually an eraser, children struggled when asked what the object looks like and what the object actually is. Moll and Tomasello also interpret these findings as evidence that children are able to *take* perspectives on an object, but are unable to combine two different perspectives on one object (i.e. that the object can be seen both as a chocolate *and* an eraser).

velopmental stage in which children are capable of generating and even using these vicarious mental files (albeit only under specific facilitating conditions) before they are able to link mental files.

Can we provide an account of the development of perspective taking using mental files? The picture for level-2 perspective taking is similar to that from the discussion of the FBT, as this requires having two representations of one object. Therefore, level-2 perspective taking requires having two mental files for one object.[8] Prior to the linking of the files this is merely a sensitivity for perspective and not perspective understanding, as perspective understanding requires an appreciation that these are two different perspectives on one and the same thing (Moll et al., 2013; Perner et al., 2002), which is not present prior to linking.

I will illustrate this using the well-known example of a 6/9 ambiguous figure. Suppose we have the setup illustrated in Figure 5.1.

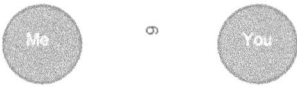

Figure 5.1: Experimental setup in a perspective taking task

In this case I see the figure as a 6, while you see the figure as a 9. Level-2 perspective taking requires being able to represent both perspectives. This means that we require two mental files (Figure 5.2.).

Regular Mental File   Vicarious Mental File

Figure 5.2: Level-2 perspective taking

These files do not have to be linked for the purposes of perspective taking, however. The linking is only required for perspective contrasting, where children need to be able to consider information from both files (Figure 5.3.).

What about level-1 perspective taking? This does not require vicarious mental files but can be done merely with one (regular) file that the other person may

---

8 Usually this would be a vicarious mental file and a regular mental file. However, there can also be perspective taking where the alternative perspective is not that of another person (e.g. past own perspective).

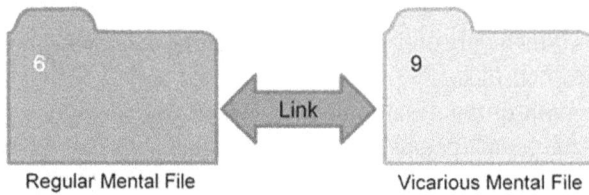

Regular Mental File   Vicarious Mental File

Figure 5.3: Level-2 perspective contrasting

or may not have access too. This could be implemented in terms of indexing but, as I will discuss below, I do not think that this 'access' is something which is explicitly represented in the file (Figure 5.4.).

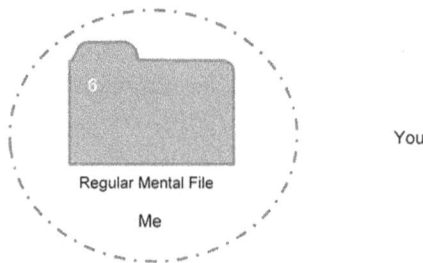

Figure 5.4: Level-1 perspective taking

Level-1 perspective taking might be contrasted with joint attention. Children show the ability to jointly attend an object at the age of 9 – 12 months. Engaging in joint attention too requires only one mental file, but this file is accessible to both oneself and the other person (Figure 5.5.).

Figure 5.5: Joint Attention

We can therefore distinguish three different stages in perspective taking using mental files. In an initial step, children develop a sensitivity to whether or not someone has access to a mental file or not (level-1 perspective taking).

From this, children are then able to create vicarious mental files, thus explicitly being able to represent a different perspective on one and the same thing (level-2 perspective taking). At this point, the child is able to take two different perspectives on one and the same thing without realising that these are perspectives on the same thing. Finally, at age 4, children develop the ability to link mental files. It is only at this point when they are able to relate perspectives to each other and realise that these are two ways of understanding the same thing that they can be credited with an *understanding* of perspective.

Why do children struggle so much with the linking of files, given that they are already able to take the perspective of another person? I want to suggest that part of the problem might be that children initially have a strongly object-focused representation. For example, in the experiment by Moll et al. (2013) children can either represent the object as being blue – "the toy is blue", or represent it as being green – "the toy is green". These two representations are conflicting – the toy cannot both be blue and green at the same time. Therefore, the two representations cannot be put together as representations of one and the same object. It is only once we move from an object-centred representation to a person-centred representation that children are able to reconcile the two perspectives. More specifically, what is required is moving from thinking "the toy is green" and "the toy is blue" to something more like "the toy is green" $_{EXPERIMENTER}$ and "the toy is blue" $_{SELF}$. To use the expression from Recanati (2012), the representations of the object have to be 'indexed' to the other person. This is not to say that prior to this indexing the representation has no connection to the other person. For example, it seems likely that there is at the very least a causal connection between the other person and the representation of their perspective. So, for example, if Sally sees the 9 on the table between us as a 6, it might be that her presence leads to my representation "6" or that the representation is activated by her appearance. Rather my point is that this is not explicitly represented as the perspective of Sally.

This move from object-focused to person-focused representations is significant not only because it allows for linking and therefore changes the way we can access perspectives.[9] It also lays the foundation for a more long-term understanding of other people and their different perspectives which maybe long lasting and independent of the situation.[10]

---

9 As argued in Chapter 4, prior to linking children are only able to access other perspectives through situational triggering. Linking allows accessing of the file with some independence from the immediate situation.

10 For example, Newen (2015) suggests that person models (or person files in our terminology) may be the central element around which social cognition comes to be organised.

The upshot of this is that, for the initial perspective taking, the child does not conceive of the perspective they are taking *as the other's* perspective.[11] It is this development in representational capacity that is required in order to be able to contrast perspectives and understand that these are different perspectives on one and the same thing and hence, it is this development which underlies perspective understanding.

5.4 Conclusion

The aim of this chapter was to further elaborate the mental files account. One of the open questions within the mental files framework concerns the nature of vicarious mental files. When and how are vicarious mental files generated? I focused in particular on the question whether in order to create vicarious mental files they must be linked to regular mental files. Concerning this, I argued in favour of the *Unlinked Account,* which states that there can be vicarious mental files that are not linked to regular mental files. I suggested two different ways in which vicarious mental files could be created without presuming a proper link to the regular mental file (Section 5.2): firstly, via directly tracking the acquaintance relations of the other person and, secondly, through a temporary information connection between regular and vicarious mental file which do not persist once the vicarious mental file is created. Postulating unlinked vicarious mental files not only allows us to explain the findings from the implicit FBT, but is also supported by some of the literature on (visual) perspective taking (Section 5.3). My final step in the next chapter will be to extend the Situational Mental File Account to children's pretend play.

---

11 It is an open question whether this would also be an upshot of Perner et al.'s (2015, Perner and Leahy, 2016) view. They clearly think that prior to being able to link mental files children do not have an understanding of perspectives, as such an understanding requires realising that the two perspectives one is representing are perspectives on one and the same object (Perner et al., 2002). However, even on his unlinked view, Perner does seem to be committed to the view that the vicarious mental file is already indexed to the other person (Perner and Brandl, 2005). Whether this is only an implicit or causal connection, as I have suggested here, or whether this indexing should be considered as representing this as the perspective of the other person (even without understanding that the other person's perspective is of the same thing as my perspective) is unclear.

6 Pretend Play and Its Importance for Mindreading

Thus far, I have mainly been concerned with the development of belief understanding and the paradox of false belief understanding. In Chapter 4, I introduced a new Situational Mental File Account to explain the paradox of false belief understanding. In Chapter 5, I then elaborated on this account, focusing on vicarious mental files and how these are created. In this chapter, I will move beyond belief attribution and the paradox of false belief understanding and look at the phenomenon of pretend play[1] in children. Pretend play is a common phenomenon in young children, with children at the age of 18 months engaging in pretend tea parties or pretending that the banana is a telephone (Leslie, 1987).

Pretend play is often thought to be closely related to belief understanding, with Alan Leslie famously arguing that children's pretence shows that children have all the prerequisite abilities required for belief understanding (Leslie, 1987, 2002). This strong claim, however, is controversial. I will focus on two elements of Leslie's argument. Firstly, Leslie argues that pretence, like belief attribution, requires the ability to form dual representations of the object. These must be kept separate from each other, lest the child confuses what is pretence and what is reality. Secondly, Leslie argues that both individual and joint pretence require the attribution of mental states to others (i.e. mindreading). If Leslie is right about these claims that pretence poses the same demands as belief attribution, then children's early pretend play generates an interesting challenge akin to the challenge posed by the implicit FBT in the paradox of false belief understanding: how do we explain children's early pretending if children are unable to pass the explicit FBT till age 4?

Focusing on the question of dual representations and whether children's pretend play requires mindreading, I will argue that the evidence from children's pretend play is not sufficient to warrant concluding that they are engaging in mindreading. Despite this, pretence remains a highly relevant phenomenon as the required duality of representations nonetheless leads to a perspective problem: the child must handle two different representations of one and the same object (the pretend representation of the object and reality). As we saw in the previous two chapters, on the mental files account, different perspectives require different files and children are only able to deal with perspective problems once they are able to link different files. If children are able to engage in pretend play

---

1 I use the terms pretend play and pretence interchangeably in this chapter.

https://doi.org/10.1515/9783110758610-010

by 18 months, but only develop the ability to link mental files at age 4, this poses a challenge for the mental files account, which is, in an interesting way, similar to the one posed by the implicit FBT. I argue that, like these types of FBT, children's pretend play can best be explained in terms of a uni-directional linking. Therefore, pretend play provides further support for the intermediate uni-directional linking stage postulated in Chapter 4.

This chapter proceeds in four steps. I begin by introducing the phenomenon of pretend play (Section 6.1.). Second, I consider whether children's early pretend play requires mindreading, where I argue that the evidence of children's early pretend play does not warrant concluding that they are mindreading (Section 6.2). Third, I argue that pretend play still poses a perspective problem and consider different ways in which the mental file account could be extended to pretend play. Specifically, I argue that the early pretence that we find in 18-month-olds is well characterised by the same situationally supported uni-directional linking which I postulated as underlying infants' success in the helping behaviour paradigm (Section 6.3). Finally, I argue that the findings from pretence can help to support and supplement the findings from the implicit FBT: even if the findings from the implicit FBT and the helping behaviour studies should not hold up, we can use evidence from pretence to show that the general account we have developed nonetheless holds true (Section 6.4).

6.1 The Core Features of Pretence

What is pretence? Pretending will be understood as intentionally acting in accordance with a situation that is known not to be the case.[2] Rakoczy (2006, 114) characterises pretence as,

> [A]t least (necessarily) acting intentionally, knowingly and non-seriously, playfully as if a counterfactual proposition was true (pretend-that) or as if really performing an action (pretend-to), but intentionally and openly stopping short of really acting as if the proposition was true or of really performing the action.

---

2 There has been some discussion whether there can be cases of true pretend. For example, Leslie (1994) points out that a child might pretend to drink from an empty plastic cup and then say that it is empty. In this case, the pretence coincides with reality. It could be argued, however, that the scenario in which this takes place is still one, which is known not to be the case. Regardless of whether there can be true pretence or not, most common cases of pretence do involve a pretend situation which is known not to be true and nothing in my discussion in this chapter hangs on this question.

For example, at a pretend tea party you may behave as if you were drinking tea from a toy cup that is empty. Similarly, when pretending to be a dog, a child might crawl on the floor in the manner of a dog. I will be focusing on early pretend play in children and therefore limit my discussion to these playful scenarios which do not involve the intention to deceive someone else.[3] To further clarify the discussion, I will highlight three criteria of pretence found in the literature, which can be derived from the definition:

1. **Duality of Representation Criterion.**[4] In order for the child to be pretending, the child must act in accordance with a state of affairs, which they know not to be true. In other words, there must be a pretend representation which differs from reality and which is "projected onto" reality (Lillard, 1994, 212; see also Leslie, 1987). Moreover, the pretender must also be aware of the distinction between pretence and reality. Minimally, this requires that the child does not confuse pretence and reality. I am not pretending that the stick is a pencil if I genuinely think the stick is a pencil.

2. **Intentionality Criterion.** Pretence is an intentional behaviour[5] (Lillard, 1994; Rakoczy, 2006, 2008a; Rakoczy et al., 2004). That is to say that in order to pretend that the stick is a pencil I must be doing so intentionally. This is to differentiate from cases where, for example, I mistake the stick for a pencil and thereby non-intentionally act as if the stick is a pencil.

3. **Epistemic Criterion.** Being able to pretend depends on having relevant background knowledge about the thing pretended. For example, in order to pretend that the stick is a pencil I must have the relevant background knowledge such as knowing what a pencil is and how it is used (Lillard, 1994; Rakoczy, 2006).[6] As I will discuss in more detail below, this criterion concerns understanding how pretence is related to other mental states, specifically knowledge.

---

3 This would broaden the scope of this chapter too much. The extent to which early deception takes place and whether this involves mindreading is a controversial topic (Perner, 1991; Reddy, 2008). To do justice to it would go beyond the scope of this chapter.

4 This is sometimes referred to as 'duality of knowledge' or 'dual knowledge' criterion. I avoid using this term, however, to avoid confusion with the third 'epistemic' criterion that deals with the relationship between pretence and previous knowledge.

5 While most people in the literature agree that pretence is a mental state, there is some debate concerning the relation between pretence and activity, and whether pretence always requires behaviour. Whether such a strong point can be made, pretence is at least closely tied to behaviour (more so than, for example, imagination, Liao and Szabó Gendler, 2011). It seems safe to say that children's understanding of pretence is closely connected to behaviour.

6 This is not required to be a propositional "knowledge that", however.

The central question in the literature is to what extent children's early pretend play fulfils these criteria. The main focus in this chapter will be on the dual representation criterion, but I also comment briefly on the other two criteria below and explain how they pertain to the debate of whether children's understanding of pretence is mentalistic or not.

6.1.1 Dual Representation Criterion

The dual representation criterion lies at the heart of Leslie's (1987) claim that pretence and belief attribution are in an important way similar to each other. The idea is that both pretence and belief attribution require dual representations which are kept separate from each other. Pretend and reality representations must be kept separate or pretend representations need to be 'quarantined' from representations of reality so that pretence does not affect children's understanding of reality. For example, when pretending that a stick is a pencil, the representation of the stick *as a pencil* must be kept separate from the child's understanding of what the stick actually is, so that the child does not come to think that the stick really is a pencil. Similarly, when observing her father pretending that the banana is a telephone, the information of the banana being used as a phone in pretence must be kept apart from the child's actual understanding of telephones and bananas, otherwise the child would come to think that the banana actually can be used for telephoning (Leslie, 1987). This is similar to belief attribution – especially false belief attribution – where one needs to keep one's own beliefs separate from the beliefs of the other person.

Most researchers – including those who argue that children do not have a mentalistic understanding of pretence – agree that children do in fact meet this criterion (Lillard, 1994; Nichols and Stich, 2000; Perner, 1991).[7] They do not become confused between pretence and reality, which means that in some way, they need to be able to keep separate information about the pretend object or scenario, and what is really the case. This alone is not sufficient, however, to conclude that pretending requires mental state attribution. Leslie (1987) suggests that mental state attribution could be a means of keeping the pretend representation separate from reality, but it is not the only way. In Section 6.2, I will argue that Leslie's further arguments in favour of the mindreading account do in fact fail to establish that children's early pretence requires attributing mental states,

---

7 Historically this has not always been the case, see Piaget (1962) who took pretending to show children's lack of a firm grip on reality.

but that the dual representations in pretence do raise a form of perspective problem and that the cognitive resources involved can be adequately described by a mental files account.

6.1.2 Intentionality Criterion

Concerning children's pretend play, one of the main questions in the literature is whether children have a mentalistic understanding of pretence. On the one extreme there are psychologists like Alan Leslie (Friedman and Leslie, 2007; Leslie, 1987, 2002) who strongly defend the view that, based on children's early pretend play at 18 months, we should credit them with a mentalistic understanding of pretence. This means that when engaging in pretence, these young children are already attributing the *mental state* of pretence to themselves and others. At the other extreme there are behavioural accounts of pretence according to which children's early pretend play is based only on a behavioural understanding of pretence (Nichols and Stich, 2000; Stich and Tarzia, 2015). In other words, children only understand pretence as a 'behaving as if' without any mentalistic component. So, for example, when the 2-year-old sees her father flapping his arms pretending to be a bird, she conceives of this as her father behaving as if he were a bird without attributing any mental states like the mental state of "pretending to be a bird" to him.

In the middle between the two extremes – at the turning point, so to speak – is the third main position of the debate, according to which children understand pretence as "intentionally acting as if". This is the view prominently defended by Rakoczy (2008a; Rakoczy and Tomasello, 2006; Rakoczy et al., 2004) who argues that the evidence may be insufficient to conclude that children have a full mentalistic understanding of pretence, but that children's early pretence already goes beyond a behavioural understanding. This means that, using the example above, the child does not yet fully understand that the father is pretending to be a bird, but does understand that he is *intentionally acting as if he were a bird*. This is an intermediate position as it does credit children with an understanding of pretence that is somewhat mentalistic: they understand the intentionality component of pretence. Nonetheless, this falls short of a fully-fledged mentalistic understanding of pretence. So, for example, children may still lack the epistemic criterion in their understanding of pretence (Rakoczy, 2006).[8]

---

8 Overall, this latter view is based on the idea that an understanding of pretence can develop gradually. This contrasts with the view held by Leslie, where the matter of understanding of pre-

Currently there is good evidence that even young children already have an intentional understanding of pretence (Rakoczy and Tomasello, 2006; Rakoczy et al., 2004). This means that they understand pretend play as a goal-oriented activity which includes an awareness of the object oneself or someone else is intentionally playing with (Woodward, 1998), i.e. the infant would be unsatisfied if the object is exchanged and the type of action it is expecting is modified (Rakoczy, 2008b). Joint pretend play, also requires joint attention in terms of the infants' ability to register that the other person is also aware of the object involved in the goal-directed action. This understanding of pretence, however, may still be limited. For example, children might not understand the difference between pretend and deception, where there is an intention to get the other person to actually hold a false belief (Rakoczy, 2008a). Similarly, children may not yet understand how pretence relates to other mental states and how it depends on one's previous knowledge (see Epistemic Criterion below). Moreover, being able to determine that someone is 'intentionally acting as if' does not require representing the perspective of the other person as such (meta-representation). I do not need to understand that he is conceiving of the stick as a pencil, just that he is behaving as if the stick is a pencil, albeit doing so intentionally.

6.1.3 Epistemic Criterion

The last – epistemic – criterion concerns how pretence relates to background knowledge and has played a role in the literature mainly in arguments against mentalistic views of pretence. In a famous study, Lillard (1993) showed children a puppet troll, Moe, who did not know anything about rabbits. Children then saw Moe hopping like a rabbit. They were asked: Is Moe pretending to be a rabbit? Children up to the age of 6 said that Moe was pretending, which Lillard took to be evidence of children's lack of a mentalistic understanding of pretence. This finding in itself was surprising, as it seemed to suggest that children's mentalistic understanding of pretence lags behind belief understanding: even children who pass the FBT still do not understand pretence. This lead Lillard (1994) to argue that there is decalage: Given that children can successfully pretend with their simpler understanding of pretence, it takes longer for this simpler understanding to be replaced than belief understanding where children struggle

---

tence is determined by whether you have a concept of pretence or not, and concepts are primitives which do not allow for gradation (Rakoczy et al., 2004). What Leslie does allow, however, is that there can be gradation in the use of the concepts.

without a proper understanding of belief. A number of methodological objections have been raised against this paradigm and the paradigm was modified (see Lillard, 2001, 1995 for a review). One important finding which sheds an interesting light onto this issue is that in an analogous task using beliefs, children also failed this kind of task until age 6 (German and Leslie, 2001). It seems, therefore, that either this task might be testing a more sophisticated aspect of understanding mental states (pretend *or* belief), or that the task confuses the children so that they fail the task even despite having the necessary understanding.

Another possibility is that children also lack an understanding of belief till the age of 6 when they pass the Moe task. This view has not been taken concerning belief understanding as the explicit FBT is generally considered to provide conclusive evidence of belief understanding.[9] However, it is also important to note that unless we take an atomistic view where partial or grades of understanding are not allowed, this issue does not need to be too pressing. There is nothing to say that children cannot have some limited early understanding of belief and pretence, which is refined further over time even after the age of 4. Indeed, it seems likely that something like this happens and that children's understanding of others, their beliefs and their pretending is refined over time.

For the remaining discussion, I will assume that even without the epistemic criterion being in place, children can have some understanding of pretence that may or may not be mentalistic in nature. I will therefore leave aside this issue and focus only on what might be called "early pretence", which is developed at around 18 months (and thus does not satisfy the epistemic criterion). This allows that there can be a more sophisticated "late pretence", which develops when children do meet the epistemic criterion and therefore have a fuller understanding of pretence. In what follows, I will use the terms pretence and pretend play to refer to this early form of pretence unless otherwise specified.

6.2 Mindreading and Pretence

To what extent does pretence require mindreading? Alan Leslie (1987, 1994, 2002) in particular has argued for a close relationship between pretence and belief attribution, claiming that the same mechanisms underlie both:

---

9 This has been alleged as an explanation of the findings from the implicit FBT, but most people agree that children do have a concept of belief at the age of 4 when they pass the explicit FBT, a notable exception being Hedger and Fabricius (2011), although their reservations are not tied to children's failure in the Moe task or the epistemic criterion.

> Pretense emerges with a mechanism that provides a specialized and powerful capacity to represent and manipulate cognitive relationships to information. The significance of this mechanism is that it constitutes a major part of the specific innate basis for the development of theory of mind. (Leslie, 1988, 24)

The main upshot of this is that Leslie argues that in pretence we can already see that the child has all she needs in order to represent beliefs and attribute them to others. This claim, however, is highly controversial (Lillard, 1993; Nichols and Stich, 2000; Perner, 1991). In this section, I will argue that the evidence from children's early pretend play does not warrant concluding that children are attributing mental states to others. I agree with Leslie, however, that in virtue of the duality of representation criterion there are important similarities between pretend play and belief attribution, which, as I will argue in Section 6.3, can be described by relying on the same mechanisms in terms of variants of linking mental files.

Let us begin by considering individual pretending, which children can engage in at 18 months. Clearly individual pretending does not require attributing mental states to anyone else, but it might require attributing mental states to oneself. One reason for thinking this, as made clear above, is that pretending requires a duality of knowledge and the child must be aware of this in order to count as pretending. To use the example from above, the child must be aware that the stick is not a pencil and nonetheless deliberately use it as a pencil, without coming to think that the stick actually is a pencil. But this awareness of the duality does not amount to needing to attribute mental states to oneself. It requires dual representations, but it is not clear that they would need to be representations of *mental states*. The different representations may be quarantined in a manner which does not require meta-representation (Perner, 1991). This would be cognitively more parsimonious and would not run into the danger of overintellectualizing the ability of pretend play.

So individual pretence does not warrant concluding that children are attributing mental states to themselves or others. But what about recognising pretence in others? Leslie's (1987) argument for the meta-representational theory of pretending is based on the finding that children begin to engage in pretence at the same time as they recognise pretence in others, that is to say that engaging in pretence and recognising pretence in others is yoked in development. Leslie does not argue that engaging in individual pretence mandates attributing mental state ascriptions to the child. Instead, he argues that their ability to recognise pretence is what warrants concluding that they are attributing mental states. It is the fact that engaging in these two abilities are yoked in development, which leads us to conclude that both pretending and recognising pretence require mindreading.

This argument has been criticised, on the grounds that the evidence of yoking in development is ambiguous and that even if the two do emerge together in development, it still does not mean that the same ability must underlie both (Jarrold et al. 1994). Furthermore, it has often been argued that even recognition of pretence in others can be explained in terms of purely recognising behaviour (Nichols and Stich, 2000; Stich and Tarzia, 2015).

I want to leave these criticisms aside for the moment, however, and consider the evidence of children's early ability to recognise pretence in more detail. Here, it is important to distinguish between joint pretence, in which the child and their partner share the same pretence, and a merely observational pretence where the child does not share the pretence of the other person. To illustrate this with an example, a case of joint pretence would be that a child and her parent had a pretend tea party together. Observational pretence would take place if the child sees the parent pretending that the cone is a cup of tea and understands this as a pretend activity, but does not herself pretend that the cone is a cup of tea.

Keeping in mind this distinction, I argue that even if observational pretence could provide evidence of mindreading – and as we have seen this is a controversial issue – joint pretence does not suffice to show that children are attributing mental states to others. In other words, if pretending requires attributing a mental state to someone else, this would only be the case for observational pretence and not for joint pretence. To see why, we need to think back to the original arguments in favour of the FBT. One of the significant advantages of the FBT is that it requires the child to attribute a mental state or perspective to another *which differs from their own*. This was needed in order to rule out that the child merely predicts the behaviour of the other from their own perspective. This distinction between the child's own perspective and another person's perspective would only be found in observational pretence and not joint pretence. Joint pretence differs from shared beliefs in that children are faced with a perspective problem (namely the dual representations of pretence and reality) which is not the case for shared beliefs (where there is just one perspective that is shared). However, this duality in joint pretence is ultimately the same as in individual pretence where the child can engage in pretence without losing track of reality. While the child does need to represent the pretence separately from reality, in joint pretence this pretence need not be attributed to anyone. As in individual pretence, the representation must be quarantined, but this need not be in the form of mental state attribution. Here the pretence could even be thought of as an impersonal or situational thing, which is happening now, rather than a perspective that must be attributed to another person. In contrast, merely observational pretence (where the child is required to recognise a pretence, which they themselves do not share) would involve a distinction between one's own perspective and that of another person. This is not to say that joint pretence cannot occur on the basis of mindreading. It could be the case that it so happens that in joint pretence children do engage in mindreading and attribute a different perspective to the other person. The point, rather, is that joint pretence does not require this and could be explained without needing to appeal to mindreading.

Most of the evidence of children's ability to recognise pretence in others comes from situations in which children engage in joint pretence with others (Bosco et al., 2006; Leslie, 1987; Rakoczy, 2006, 2007; Rakoczy et al., 2005). Children are able to understand what the experimenter is doing and respond to this appropriately given the pretend scenario. But this response is within the context of the pretend play itself and therefore based on pretend representations that the child shares with the experimenter.

It might be objected here that the distinction between joint pretence and observational pretence is an artificial one. After all, in order to engage in joint pretence, the child might need to first observe the pretence and only once they have understood it can they join in and adopt the pretence for themselves. However, joint pretence is different from merely observational pretence, as the child at no point has to distinguish between their own perspective and that of another person. Even in the initial recognition of the pretence, the child does not have to attribute the perspective specifically to the other person. All they have to do is determine the *contents* of the pretence to be shared, rather than attributing the pretence to that person and only then adopting it for themselves. Thinking back to the different levels of perspective taking introduced in Chapter 5, pretence may require generating an alternative perspective, but it does not require contrasting another's perspective with one's own. Moreover, it does not require representing the pretend perspective *as the perspective of the other person*. A further difference between joint pretence and observational pretence is that the understanding of pretence required for the joint pretence is an immediate interactive one, rather than a detached reflective understanding.

Where does this leave us? It seems that the evidence from pretence is not strong enough to decisively show that pretending requires mindreading. But, even though early pretend play does not require mindreading, it still poses a perspective problem. This notion of a perspective problem is not limited to mental state attribution, but also covers phenomena like alternative naming (Doherty and Perner, 2020; Perner et al., 2002). Even in their early pretend play, children do meet the duality of representation criterion. Moreover, children keep the information about pretence and reality separate. This means that even though children may not need to represent the perspective of the other person, they do have to deal with the dual perspectives of pretend and reality. In order to engage in individual pretence, as well as joint pretence, the child needs to come to understand the content of the pretend play episode. This content must diverge from what is actually the case and the child must be able to maintain this distinction – that is to say, they must not get confused about reality and pretence. Let us return to the example of the child pretending that this stick is a pencil. It is agreed that even 18-month-old children who engage in this kind of play do not come to think that the stick actually is a pencil and attribute properties of the pencil (e.g. used for writing) to the stick. This means that in this pretend play the information about the 'stick pencil' must be kept separate from the child's normal knowledge of the stick and how it works. Putting this in terms of mental files, in order for the child to not lose their proper understanding of sticks, the original stick file must remain intact. Given that files are a means of collecting and integrating knowledge on an object, this suggests that pretence requires co-referential files for the stick – a file for the pretence and a regular mental file for reality. The open question, which I will be addressing in Section 6.3., is how these files are related to each other: are they merely two distinct files, or is there evidence of linking between them?

In the next section, I will extend the Situational Mental File Account and argue that pretend play, like the evidence from the active helping behaviour paradigms, is best explained in terms of uni-directional linking. This allows us to preserve the intuition that there is a genuine development in belief understanding which takes place at the age of 4, but allows that children have some abilities in dealing with different perspectives prior to this point already.

6.3 Extending the Mental Files Account

As we saw in the previous section, pretence, like mindreading, depends on dual representations and therefore poses a perspective problem in the wide sense introduced by Perner et al. (2002). While, unlike mindreading, pretence does not require taking the perspective of another person, it does require being able to take different perspectives on one and the same object (e.g. what the object really is and what I pretend the object is). Therefore, drawing a connection to pretence on this basis is unproblematic, even if early pretence does not involve the attribution of mental states to others.

To be clear about the dialectics of this discussion, given that pretend play poses a perspective problem, I take it that it poses a challenge for any account of belief attribution in terms of mental files, as this account focuses on belief attribution as a perspective problem. I have argued in Chapter 4 that the mental files framework is a useful tool for thinking about cognitive development and have shown that it can be used to develop an explanation of the paradox of false belief understanding. Given my use of mental files as a promising means for thinking about cognitive development, my primary aim is therefore to argue that this account can be extended to also account for cases of early pretend play. The dual perspectives involved make pretend play relevant for mental files accounts in terms of posing a challenge for when children are able to *have* and *link* co-referential files. Pretend play is especially significant here, because children are able to engage in pretence at the age of 18 months already (Liao and Szabó Gendler, 2011), and not only at 4 when the ability for full linking develops (Doherty and Perner, 2020; Perner and Leahy, 2016; Perner et al., 2002). An account of belief attribution in terms of linking between mental files should also be able to tell a story about pretend play as both pose a similar kind of perspective problem. Thus far, no such account has been put forward in the literature.

That being said, pretend play does not only pose a challenge for a mental files account of belief attribution, it also provides an opportunity. As I have argued, pretend play provides further evidence of children's early abilities to maintain dual representations of one and the same thing and we can use this in order to strengthen the arguments concerning the interpretation of the findings from the implicit FBT.

How can we extend the Situational Mental File Account developed in Chapter 4 to cover pretend play? One difference in the case of both individually pretending and recognising pretence to belief attribution is that we do not need a vicarious mental file that represents the object from another person's perspective. This is because the pretend representation is something that the child herself adopts, albeit in a limited manner that is constrained to the pretend context. We therefore do not need to posit vicarious mental files in order to make sense of early pretence. At the same time, however, the pretence also cannot merely be represented in a regular mental file, as this would not allow the child to distinguish between pretence and reality. The file must therefore be marked in some way as a pretend mental file, akin to a vicarious mental file in that it is segregated from the regular mental files and therefore allows for storage of information for pretend play, without endangering the child's understanding of reality.

How are pretend mental files generated? I will illustrate this using the example of a child pretending that a wooden block is a car. The child will have a regular mental file of the wooden block (Figure 6.1).

The pretend representation is copied from the child's representation of a car. While the normal 'car' file is anchored in a car, the pretend 'car' file is anchored

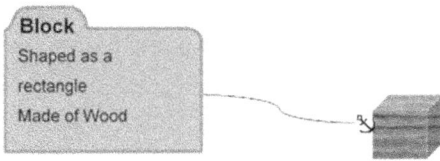

Figure 6.1: Regular mental file of the block.

in the same wooden block as the 'block' file, such that these files are now co-referential (Figure 6.2).

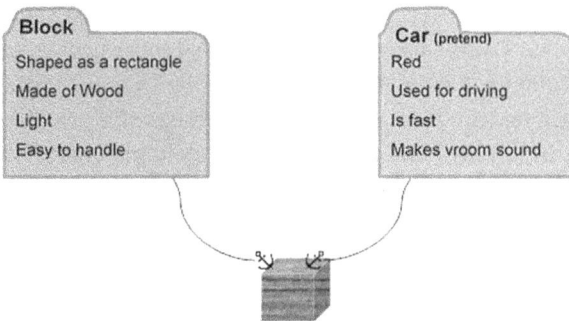

Figure 6.2: Regular mental file for the block and the pretend mental file of the car both anchored in the same object.

A different kind of pretence, which is commonly found in addition to object substitution is property substitution, is when a child attributes properties to an object that it does not actually have in pretence. [10] For example, the child might pretend that the wooden block is really heavy and cannot be lifted, even though

---

10 Leslie (1987) notes a further kind of pretence, namely pretending the existence of non-existent entities. This kind of a pretence does not make use of props. This would require a slightly different model as the duality would have to be represented in a different manner, as there is no currently present object to anchor in. Consider a child pretending that there is a tiger in the living room. The representational duality must still be maintained as the child pretends that there is a tiger in the living room while at the same time knowing that there is not really a tiger in the living room. What makes this kind of pretence different is that it requires being able to represent absences and it has not yet been worked out how this is done on a mental files account. In the example given here, this might be represented in terms of two living room files, with the pretend mental file containing the information that there is a tiger. This kind of pretence seems to develop later than the previous more object centred two (Rakoczy, 2006) and I will therefore not consider it further here.

it is actually very light (Figure 6.3). In this case, the pretend mental file is copied from the regular mental file of the block, but some of the properties are exchanged:

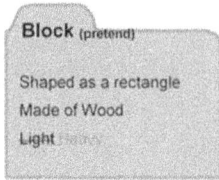

Block (pretend)

Shaped as a rectangle
Made of Wood
Light Heavy

Figure 6.3: Property substitution pretence. Pretend mental file is derived from the regular mental file with some of the information changed.

Where do these new properties come from? Perhaps from another object that is heavy, for example a gold bar. I want to suggest, however, that these new properties are generated in the context of a *situation model*. Take the example of the full cup, this kind of pretence usually comes about in the context of a situation like a pretend tea party, for which there are scripts that mandate the change in properties of the objects due to causal chains which are acted out like 'pouring' tea into the cup. Similarly, the 'heavy block' might come about in a game with a super strong hero who can lift things which normal people cannot.

One thing highlighted by the discussion of pretence is the limitations of talking only in terms of mental files of *objects*. In pretence, but also in belief attribution, our concern is usually not only with objects, but also with whole situations and scenarios. Children pretend to have a tea party, not just that the cup is full, and behavioural scripts may follow from these scenarios. This is not to say that mental files of objects do not play an important role in pretence, but merely to say that pretence, even in young children, goes beyond single objects. A child may pretend that a block is a car and then, from this, carry out a pretend visit to the wooden box that is the 'garage', including some of the procedures she might have observed at a recent visit to the garage. Therefore, although I have previously spoken only in terms of mental files for objects, the mental files account should not be seen as being limited to representations of objects, but also include representations of situations, persons and even groups (Newen, 2015). In a similar direction, Hommel (2004) presents evidence that our representations may also be structured as 'event files' which contain not only the features of objects but link these with a wider context including especially behavioural responses. On this picture, mental files for objects are only a sub-component of broader event files.

Having discussed how the pretend mental file is generated, let us now turn to the linking of files. What is the nature of the linking between the pretend mental file and the regular mental file? As in the case of mindreading, in pretence there are two mental files that are anchored in the same object: the pretend mental file of the car and the regular mental file of the block are both anchored in the block. How do these two files relate to each other?

One possibility would be that the mental files are initially unlinked. Therefore, like in the looking behaviour implicit FBTs, which file is activated would depend solely on situational factors: if the pretend context is emphasised, then children will activate the pretend mental file, if the real state of affairs is emphasised, then children will activate the regular mental file. What this would mean is that the regular mental file of the object plays no role in pretence. One consideration that speaks against such a clear segregation is that even in the pretend context children do not seem to forget the real nature and function of the object. They do not come to think that the block really is a car. There are, however, two ways, in which this might be achieved: firstly, through some form of linking to the regular mental file which allows the child to maintain a grip on reality even in the context of pretend play, or secondly, through a feature of the pretend mental file itself, for example if there is only limited information in the file and its application is constrained to only very particular contexts. Note, however, that the latter would require a form of meta-awareness. Although this meta-awareness might seem like a very demanding condition, it is possible that children meet this condition given that pre-schoolers are at least able to label pretence as such, even though they do not do so regularly till age 5 (Lillard and Witherington, 2004). Note also that these two proposals need not be mutually exclusive: the marking of the pretend mental file may well be achieved through a particular kind of linking with the regular mental file that is constrained in some manner.

Another possibility is that there is a full linking between the pretend and regular mental files. This would mean that children are liberally able to move between pretend and regular mental files at will and independently of situational factors. This proposal is especially interesting because, if true, it would cast some doubt on the account I proposed concerning mindreading. If children are already able to fully link pretend mental files and regular mental files at 18 months, why are they unable to do so with regular and vicarious mental files? This might suggest, contrary to what is argued by Perner et al. (2002), that there is an added difficulty in processing the perspective of another person as opposed to dealing with two perspectives on an object per se, or that inhibiting one's own perspective over the perspective of another person requires higher levels of inhibition than inhibiting reality in favour of pretence. The critical prediction of this proposal would be that children could move from the regular mental file to the pretend mental file independently of situational factors.

Currently, however, there is no evidence, which necessitates concluding that children are able to do this. While children do engage in pretence and have considerable competence in this, early pretence often takes place in the context of *joint pretence*, usually in the presence of an adult who provides the situational context for pretence (Rakoczy, 2006). In experiments testing pretence, the set-up is usually that children are introduced to a particular pretence scenario and are then tested on their ability to act in accordance with it (Bosco et al., 2006; Leslie, 1987; Rakoczy, 2006, 2007; Rakoczy et al., 2005).

But what about individual pretence? Does this not require full linking? This would be the case if young children were regularly to take up objects with very established uses and pretend something with them which they had not encountered before as this would require a link from regular mental file (e. g. is a stick) to vicarious mental file (e. g. is a pencil). But actually the evidence of early individual pretence tends to be with toy objects which children have probably used in pretence with others before (Rakoczy, 2006). If these objects have become associated with pretence in the past, the object itself may come to cue the pretend mental file. This would be especially true of objects such as toy cups whose primary purpose is to be used in pretend play.

This leaves the possibility that there is a uni-directional linking between the pretend mental file and the regular mental file. This would mean that infants are able to move from the pretend mental file to the regular mental file, but not vice versa. On this view, the pretend mental file could only be activated by situational factors. At first sight, it might seem that on this view the pretend mental file never would be activated because the child is faced with the real object. It is important to remember, however, that the situation involves more than just the object. In particular, play partners may play a crucial role in setting up the pretend situation and therefore provide crucial scaffolding for the child. Joint pretence in this context may be crucial, and there is evidence that joint pretence may be the earliest emerging form of pretence (Rakoczy, 2006, 2007; Rakoczy et al., 2005) with children's pretence emerging strongly in joint pretence with siblings where usually the sibling sets up the pretence and the child begins imitating the pretend actions (Dunn and Dale, 1984; Perner et al., 1994). Moreover, as mentioned above, in experiments testing pretence in young children it is usually the case that it is the experimenter who sets up the pretend scenario which the child then joins in (Bosco et al., 2006; Leslie, 1987; Rakoczy, 2006, 2007; Rakoczy et al., 2005). Furthermore, it is important not to forget the role that desires play in pretence. The child might form the desire to play with a 'car' and this desire can then highlight the pretend mental file increasing the chance that is it activated. This would not be a purely situational factor anymore, but rather an example of a change in an internal state that highlights certain features of the environment.

Overall, there is some evidence that suggests that pretend and regular mental files are not completely unlinked, but there is currently no evidence to suggest that young children, when they first begin pretending are able to move from a regular mental file to a pretend mental file independently of situational factors. Therefore, the evidence from pretend play is in line with the account of uni-directional linking. Making the prediction from this account clear, I predict that when children first start pretending at 18 months, they are able to pretend following situational cueing of the pretend mental file. What I predict they are unable to do, is engage in pretence when the regular mental file has been highlighted. For example, they would not use the banana phone in an 'eating context' (at least if this pretence has not already been commonly established). Similarly, they struggle to initiate novel and creative pretence without the support of a pretend play partner. Specifically, I predict that if a child is told that they are having a tea party, "Can you pass me your cup?", they would successfully be able to pick up a suitable object to pretend that it is their cup (a cube, for example) and act appropriately with it. What they would struggle with, however, is if they are given a cube without the pretend context being set up and asked to pretend with it. In this case, I predict children would be unable to draw on a suitable pretend mental file given the lack of situation facilitation. This ability to take an object and come up with a possible pretence with it is something that only develops later when bi-directional linking is available.

6.4 The Implicit and Explicit Distinction and the Role of Situational Factors

The findings from the implicit FBT have been hit hard by the replication crisis including, in particular, the findings from the helping behaviour paradigm. The results are mixed, with some studies replicating some of the initial findings from Buttelmann et al. (2009), though this is often only partial and usually with less impressive strength (Barone et al., 2019; Kulke and Rakoczy, 2018). In particular the true belief condition has proven hard to replicate (e. g. Priewasser et al. 2018). Overall, the implicit FBT, including the helping behaviour paradigm, should be seen as "fragile paradigms" (Rubio-Fernández, 2018, 317), which is perhaps not too surprising given that I have argued that they are highly context sensitive. Nonetheless, there is a worry that this might make a theory seem unfalsifiable: if an experiment fails, it must be because of some failed situational facilitation. Such explanations can be found, but in the lack of clear, pre-defined criteria of what exactly motivates a shift of attention in the child, these explanations may appear post hoc. One of the reasons why I highlight pretend play is that it allows us to further support this implicit/explicit distinction, and especially the intermediate stage of uni-directional linking which I argued for in Chapter 4.

Firstly, children are engaging in and recognise pretence at the age of around 18 months (Leslie, 1987; Liao and Szabó Gendler, 2011).[11] This is around the age at which children have been shown to pass the helping behaviour task. If, as I have argued, the same representational demands underlie pretence as the FBT, then this would support the idea of an early implicit level of mindreading. If the same functions underlie pretence as the FBT, then children demonstrate the necessary capacities in the context of sufficient situational facilitation at 18 months, even if the findings from the helping behaviour paradigm do not replicate.

Moreover, there is evidence of an implicit-explicit distinction even in pretence (Wyman et al., 2009). Most studies looking at the emergence of pretence have made use of behavioural measures: does the child pretend? Does the child's behaviour match the pretend scenario, which has been set up by the examiner? Studies looking at children's understanding of pretence, especially by those who are sceptical of the rich view of children's understanding of pretence, have used verbal measures to test children's understanding of pretence. Interestingly, when comparing children's performance in pretence understanding for using both behavioural (implicit) measures and verbal (explicit) measures, Wyman et al. found that young children of age 3 were already successful in implicit versions of the task, while they did not pass explicit versions of the task. This seems to suggest that, rather than being a precursor of belief understanding, pretence actually shows the same developmental trajectory as belief attribution, the main difference being in the means of testing. Evidence for early pretence has usually come from behavioural studies in which children's behaviour is strongly situationally scaffolded and embedded within a context, while belief attribution has typically been tested verbally in a less strongly situationally scaffolded context.

This brings me to the second use of pretence for my argument: namely, that children's early success in pretending and recognising pretence seems to lend support to the role of situational factors and how these can compensate for a missing component of cognitive development. I have argued that in pretence

---

11 There is evidence that children may have some basic pretend abilities even earlier (Liao and Szabó Gendler, 2011).

we see some of the same cognitive demands on the child as in mindreading. Pretending is a strongly situationally scaffolded activity through the use of props and especially play partners. Early pretence is primarily joint pretence in which the child largely follows the lead of the caregiver (Haight and Miller, 1992; Rakoczy, 2007; Slade, 1987). The caregiver introduces the scenario and guides the play, thereby strongly cuing the pretend representation that is required in the absence of full linking. There is evidence that both more abstract (i.e. using props with less similarity to the pretend object or even not requiring a prop) and more creative play is something that only develops later (Rakoczy et al., 2005). This seems to suggest that early pretend play takes place predominantly in situations where there is strong situational support to scaffold the pretence. Pretend play is a cognitively demanding task, having a strong situational scaffolding may reduce demands enabling children to engage in pretend play earlier than they would be able to do otherwise.

This suggestion is very much in line with the account I have been developing, where performance is determined by a combination of situational and cognitive factors. Situational support can reduce some of the load on cognitive processes, thereby allowing (within limits) for early successful performance. However, it is only once further cognitive development has occurred that children are able to achieve success without situational support. Applying this to pretend play, this means that children would be capable of early, situationally supported pretend play, but that pretend play which does not have such support (e.g. more pretend without props) does not occur till later in development.

6.5 Conclusion

In this chapter, I have extended the Situational Mental File Account to consider children's early pretend play. The aim of this was to provide further support for the intermediate uni-directional linking stage, which was postulated in Chapter 4 in order to explain the findings from the active helping behaviour paradigms.

Children's pretend play has long since been of interest to researchers as being closely related to belief attribution. In this chapter, I argued that pretend play falls short of providing evidence of early mindreading, however it remains an interesting phenomenon from the perspective of the Situational Mental File Account as pretence still poses a perspective problem: children must manage different perspectives on one and the same object, even if these are not the perspectives of different people. In terms of mental files, this means that children's early pretence also involves co-referential mental files, even though it does not require vicarious mental files. I argued that there is reason to think that these co-referential mental files are linked via uni-directional linking in pretend play, providing further support of a uni-directional linking stage. Although children's early pretend play has been much less extensively researched than belief understanding, it is an interesting phenomenon that poses some similar demands to belief understanding and can potentially supplement the findings from the FBT, especially the findings from the implicit FBT that have been brought into question in the course of the replication crisis.

In conclusion, although pretend play does not require mindreading, it does require coordinating co-referential mental files and provides further evidence of an early and limited situationally supported linking between co-referential files.

Conclusions and Outlook

In the previous chapters, I argued for the Situational Mental File Account as a new and empirically adequate account of the paradox of false belief understanding. The central idea of the account I have been developing is that children begin with a very strongly situation-dependent sensitivity for other people's perspective. They pass the implicit FBT in virtue of situational support. Through cognitive development over time, children achieve a level of independence of the situational influences, allowing them to also succeed in situations with less situational facilitation, such as the explicit FBT. Importantly, I have outlined how this cognitive development is itself strongly driven by situational factors. I implemented this within the mental files framework, arguing that children start with unlinked mental files, which can be activated due to situational factors. Through the development of the ability to link mental files, which allows for some independence from the immediate situational context, children gradually extend the flexibility of their ability to attribute beliefs to others. In conclusion, I want to highlight three of the main contributions of this account to the debate on social cognition and the development of belief understanding.

Firstly, by making use of the mental files framework (Perner et al., 2015; Perner and Leahy, 2016; Recanati, 2012) I was able to provide a detailed account of the cognitive development underlying the paradox of false belief understanding and the role that situational factors play within this development. While there have been previous accounts using mental files to explain specifically how children come to pass the explicit FBT at age 4 (Perner et al., 2015; Perner and Leahy, 2016), I substantially extended these accounts in two ways: i) considering how this cognitive development relates to situational factors, and ii) providing an explanation for the findings from the implicit FBT. One of the key predictions of the Situational Mental File Account is that at the early stages of development where children are not able to link mental files, task performance will depend largely on whether the task emphasises the perspective of the other person or not. Young infants perform well on the implicit FBTs because these tasks do place such a continuous emphasis on the other person. If we modify the implicit FBT, however, to place an emphasis on reality, then children's performance should get worse. Similarly, children struggle with the explicit FBT because these tasks often introduce a focus on reality. If the task is modified to emphasise the perspective of the other person, performance should improve. Whether the task is implicit or explicit does not determine performance as much as the situational factors underlying the task emphasising the perspective of the other person.

https://doi.org/10.1515/9783110758610-011

Secondly, the Situational Mental File Account is novel in introducing an intermediate uni-directional linking stage in order to explain the findings from the active helping behaviour paradigms. As I argued in Chapter 2, there are reasons to think that these active behavioural FBT paradigms tap into a more advanced ability than the classic looking behaviour FBTs as they already require children to relate the other person's perspective to their own knowledge of reality. Nonetheless, there remains a difference between this stage and the later stage at age 4 where children are able to pass the explicit FBT. By postulating a uni-directional linking stage I was able to account for these findings, thereby extending the mental files account to also cover the different findings from the implicit FBTs. As I argued in Chapter 6, this uni-directional linking stage also allows us to explain the findings from children's early pretend play, thereby providing further support for such a uni-directional linking stage.

This suggestion of uni-directional linking is new within the literature on mental files and opens new avenues of research. For example, in their work on mental files, Perner et al. (2015) often allude to similarities between the FBT and the alternative naming task, both of which require linking in order to pass the task. It would be interesting, therefore, to see whether we could find a similar uni-directional linking stage also within the alternative naming task. For example, it could be that children are able to link back to basic level terms (e. g. bird) following the naming of the non-base level term (e. g. 'animal') but not vice versa. Further research is therefore needed to explore whether there are further contexts in which we can find such uni-directional linking in order to establish whether this is a general phenomenon of linking or not.

Thirdly, I elaborated on previous mental file accounts by actively defending the view that there can be unlinked mental files. In other words, this means that children are sensitive to and able to represent the perspective of others before relating this perspective to their own. This is significant as there is some debate in the literature whether there can be unlinked vicarious mental files. Furthermore, this account has implications for broader theories of social understanding. Here we can differentiate between first person priority accounts (e. g. Goldman, 2006) and third person priority accounts (e. g. Carruthers, 2009). According to the first person priority account, our understanding of others derives from our understanding of our own mental states. On the third person priority account, we have a third person understanding of mental states which we use for both understanding others and ourselves. On the view I developed in Chapter 5, our understanding of perspectives that underlies the understanding of beliefs, depends on the interdependence of both the first person experience of having a perspective as well as the ability to take the perspective of the other person. It is through combining the first person 'having a perspective' and the third person 'taking a perspective' that an understanding of perspectives is achieved. A more detailed account of this and its implications would need to be spelled out in future research.

The account I have been developing is one specifically about the development of belief understanding in the context of the FBT. Although I have expanded the account to also consider perspective taking more broadly and children's early pretence, it must be remembered that this is only a small part of our much wider social cognition ability. As I argued in Chapter 1, belief attribution is an important component of both mindreading and social cognition more generally. Nonetheless, it remains only one component of a larger picture, and one avenue of future research would be to explore to what extent the Situational Mental File Account can be extended to further components of social cognition. This could take place at three different levels.

Firstly, concerning belief attribution, I have been looking at the development of belief understanding up to age 4. Children's understanding of belief and their ability to apply this understanding continues to develop past this point, as is shown for example by children only passing second order FBTs at age 5 or later (Miller, 2009; Perner and Wimmer, 1985). A future avenue of research would be to explore whether the Situational Mental File Account can also be used to provide an explanation of these later findings.

Secondly, it would be interesting to investigate whether the Situational Mental File Account can accommodate other forms of mindreading such as the attribution of desires. While desires are fairly similar to beliefs, their relation to reality is different. Representing someone's desires may therefore require a different kind of vicarious file to belief attribution, or there may be a different kind of linking at play. Considering how the account might be extended also to desires is especially significant given that children tend to develop an understanding of diverging desires before understanding diverging beliefs (Rakoczy et al., 2007). Wellman and Liu (2004) have argued that we find a developmental Theory of Mind scale, according to which children are first able to understand knowledge and ignorance, before diverging desires and finally diverging beliefs. Although the question of whether we really find a uniform pattern of development here is controversial, and there is evidence of cultural variation (e. g. Duh et al., 2016), it would be interesting to see if the Situational Mental File account could be extended to explain this developmental scale. For example, it is possible that in order to understand another person's knowledge or ignorance no vicarious mental files are needed. All that is needed is tracking whether someone has access to the mental file or not (akin to level 1 perspective taking, as discussed in Section 5.3). A question to be addressed is whether vicarious mental files are required for understanding desires, or whether diverging desires are represented in an alternative manner, given that they do not aim to represent the world as it is. One possibility here is that vicarious mental files may be required in order to represent desires, but the nature of their linking to the regular file (i. e. one's own representation of reality) is different than the linking we find with regards to belief, given that desires do not have to represent reality. This, however, would need to be worked out in much more detail in further research.

Lastly, more broadly speaking, how does the Situational Mental File Account fit into a pluralist picture where there are multiple strategies of social cognition beyond mindreading? These include, for example, predicting the behaviour of others based on behavioural scripts or past behaviour. Some recent pluralist accounts of social cognition have argued that our understanding of others is based on models (Spaulding, 2018) or more specifically 'person models' and 'situation models' (Newen, 2015). One promising avenue of research may therefore be to consider the role of the Situational Mental File Account and the ability to represent different perspectives within such a broader 'person model'. Integrating the Situational Mental File Account within a wider account of social cognition would be an important task for future research.

Bibliography

Amsterlaw, J., and Wellman, H. M. (2006). Theories of Mind in Transition: A Microgenetic Study of the Development of False Belief Understanding. *Journal of Cognition and Development*, 7(2), 139–172. https://doi.org/10.1207/s15327647jcd0702_1

Andrews, K. (2012). *Do Apes Read Minds? Toward a New Folk Psychology*. Cambridge, M.A.: MIT Press. https://doi.org/10.5860/choice.50-3188

Andrews, K. (2017). Pluralistic Folk Psychology in Humans and Other Apes. In J. Kiverstein (Ed.), *Routledge Handbook of the Philosophy of the Social Mind*, 117–138. New York: Routledge. https://doi.org/10.4324/9781315530178

Apperly, I. A. (2011). *Mindreaders: The Cognitive Basis of Theory of Mind*. Hove: Psychology Press.

Apperly, I. A., and Butterfill, S. A. (2009). Do Humans Have Two Systems to Track Beliefs and Belief-like States? *Psychological Review*, 116(4), 953–970. https://doi.org/10.1037/a0016923

Apperly, I. A., Riggs, K. J., Simpson, A., Chiavarino, C., and Samson, D. (2006). Is Belief Reasoning Automatic? *Psychological Science*, 17(10), 841–844. https://doi.org/10.1111/j.1467-9280.2006.01791.x

Arora, A., Weiss, B., Schurz, M., Aichhorn, M., Wieshofer, R. C., and Perner, J. (2015). Left Inferior-parietal Lobe Activity in Perspective Tasks: Identity Statements. *Frontiers in Human Neuroscience*, 9(June), 1–17. https://doi.org/10.3389/fnhum.2015.00360

Avramides, A. (2001). *Other Minds*. London: Routledge.

Back, E., and Apperly, I. A. (2010). Two Sources of Evidence on the Non-automaticity of True and False Belief Ascription. *Cognition*, 115(1), 54–70. https://doi.org/10.1016/j.cognition.2009.11.008

Baillargeon, R., Buttelmann, D., and Southgate, V. (2018). Invited Commentary: Interpreting Failed Replications of Early False-belief Findings: Methodological and Theoretical Considerations. *Cognitive Development*, 46(May), 112–124. https://doi.org/10.1016/j.cogdev.2018.06.001

Baillargeon, R., Scott, R. M., and He, Z. (2010). False-belief Understanding in Infants. *Trends in Cognitive Sciences*, 14(3), 110–118. https://doi.org/10.1016/j.tics.2009.12.006

Baker, S. T., Leslie, A. M., Gallistel, C. R., and Hood, B. M. (2016). Bayesian Change-point Analysis Reveals Developmental Change in a Classic Theory of Mind Task. *Cognitive Psychology*, 91, 124–149. https://doi.org/10.1016/j.cogpsych.2016.08.001

Baron-Cohen, S. (1995). *Mindblindness: An Essay on Autism and Theory of Mind*. Cambridge, M.A.: MIT Press.

Baron-Cohen, S., Leslie, A. M., and Frith, U. (1985). The Autistic Child Have a "Theory of Mind"? *Cognitive Development*, 21, 37–46. https://doi.org/10.1016/0010-0277(85)90022-8

Barone, P., Corradi, G., and Gomila, A. (2019). Infants' Performance in Spontaneous-response False Belief Tasks: A Review and Meta-analysis. *Infant Behavior and Development*, 57, 101350. https://doi.org/10.1016/j.infbeh.2019.

Bartsch, K., and Wellman, H. M. (1995). *Children Talk About the Mind*. New York: Oxford University Press.

Bennett, J. (1978). Some Remarks About Concepts. *Behavioral and Brain Sciences*, 1(4), 557–560. https://doi.org/10.1017/S0140525X00076573

https://doi.org/10.1515/9783110758610-012

Berio, L. (2020). Culturally Embedded Schemata for False Belief Reasoning. *Synthese.* https://doi.org/10.1007/s11229-020-02655-7

Birch, S. A. J., and Bloom, P. (2007). The Curse of Knowledge in Reasoning About False Beliefs. *Psychological Science, 18*(5), 382–386. https://doi.org/10.1111/j.1467-9280.2007.01909.x

Bosco, F. M., Friedman, O., and Leslie, A. M. (2006). Recognition of Pretend and Real Actions in Play by 1- and 2-year-Olds: Early Success and Why They Fail. *Cognitive Development, 21*(1), 3–10. https://doi.org/10.1016/j.cogdev.2005.09.006

Bosco, F. M., Gabbatore, I., and Tirassa, M. (2014). A Broad Assessment of Theory of Mind in Adolescence: The Complexity of Mindreading. *Consciousness and Cognition, 24*, 84–97. https://doi.org/10.1016/j.concog.2014.01.003

Bradford, E. E. F., Jentzsch, I., and Gomez, J. C. (2015). From Self to Social Cognition: Theory of Mind Mechanisms and Their Relation to Executive Functioning. *Cognition, 138*, 21–34. https://doi.org/10.1016/j.cognition.2015.02.001

Buckner, C. (2014). The Semantic Problem(s) with Research on Animal Mind-Reading. *Mind and Language, 29*(5), 566–589. https://doi.org/10.1111/mila.12066

Burge, T. (2018). Do Infants and Nonhuman Animals Attribute Mental States? *Psychological Review, 125*(3), 409–434. https://doi.org/10.1037/rev0000091

Buttelmann, D., Buttelmann, F., Carpenter, M., Call, J., and Tomasello, M. (2017). Great Apes Distinguish True from False Beliefs in an Interactive Helping Task. *PLoS ONE, 12*(4), 1–13. https://doi.org/10.1371/journal.pone.0173793

Buttelmann, D., Carpenter, M., and Tomasello, M. (2009). Eighteen-month-old Infants Show False Belief Understanding in an Active Helping Paradigm. *Cognition, 112*(2), 337–342. https://doi.org/10.1016/j.cognition.2009.05.006

Buttelmann, F., Suhrke, J., and Buttelmann, D. (2015). What You Get Is What You Believe: Eighteen-month-olds Demonstrate Belief Understanding in an Unexpected-identity task. *Journal of Experimental Child Psychology, 131*, 94–103. https://doi.org/10.1016/j.jecp.2014.11.009

Butterfill, S. A. (2013). Interacting Mindreaders. *Philosophical Studies, 165*(3), 841–863. https://doi.org/10.1007/s11098-012-9980-x

Butterfill, S. A., and Apperly, I. A. (2013). How to Construct a Minimal Theory of Mind. *Mind and Language, 28*(5), 606–637. https://doi.org/10.1111/mila.12036

Camerer, C., Loewenstein, G., and Weber, M. (1989). The Curse of Knowledge in Economic Settings: An Experimental Analysis. *Journal of Political Economy, 97*(5), 1232–1254. https://doi.org/10.1086/261651

Carruthers, P. (1996). Simulation and Self-knowledge: A Defence of the Theory-theory. In P. Carruthers and P. K. Smith (Eds.), *Theories of Theories of Mind*, 22–68. Cambridge: Cambridge University Press.

Carruthers, P. (2009). How We Know Our Own Minds: The Relationship Between Mindreading and Metacognition. *Behavioral and Brain Sciences, 32*(2), 121–182. https://doi.org/10.1017/S0140525X09000545

Carruthers, P. (2013). Mindreading in Infancy. *Mind and Language, 28*(2), 141–172. https://doi.org/10.1111/mila.12014

Carruthers, P. (2016). Two Systems for Mindreading? *Review of Philosophy and Psychology, 7*(1), 141–162. https://doi.org/10.1007/s13164-015-0259-y

Carruthers, P. (2020). Representing the Mind as Such in Infancy. *Review of Philosophy and Psychology*. https://doi.org/10.1007/s13164-020-00491-9

Cassidy, K. W., Fineberg, D. S., Brown, K., and Perkins, A. (2005). Theory of Mind May Be Contagious, but You Don't Catch It from Your Twin. *Child Development*, 76(1), 97–106. https://doi.org/doi:10.1111/j.1467-8624.2005.00832.x

Chun, M. M. (2000). Contextual Cueing of Visual Attention. *Trends in Cognitive Sciences*, 4(5), 170–178. https://doi.org/10.1016/S1364-6613(00)01476-5

Clark, A., and Chalmers, D. (1998). The Extended Mind. *Analysis*, 58(1), 7–19. https://doi.org/10.1093/analys/58.1.7

Clements, W. A., and Perner, J. (1994). Implicit Understanding of Belief. *Cognitive Development*, 9(4), 377–395. https://doi.org/10.1016/0885-2014(94)90012-4

Davidson, D. (1963). Actions, Reasons, and Causes. *The Journal of Philosophy*, 60(23), 685–700. https://doi.org/10.2307/2023177

de Bruin, L. C., and Kästner, L. (2012). Dynamic Embodied Cognition. *Phenomenology and the Cognitive Sciences*, 11(4), 541–563. https://doi.org/10.1007/s11097-011-9223-1

de Bruin, L. C., and Newen, A. (2012). An Association Account of False Belief Understanding. *Cognition*, 123(2), 240–259. https://doi.org/10.1016/j.cognition.2011.12.016

de Bruin, L. C., and Newen, A. (2014). The Developmental Paradox of False Belief Understanding: A Dual-system Solution. *Synthese*, 191(3), 297–320. https://doi.org/10.1007/s11229-012-0127-6

De Jaegher, H., Di Paolo, E., and Gallagher, S. (2010). Can Social Interaction Constitute Social Cognition? *Trends in Cognitive Sciences*, 14(10), 441–447. https://doi.org/10.1016/j.tics.2010.06.009

de Villiers, J. G., and de Villiers, P. A. (2014). The Role of Language in Theory of Mind Development. *Topics in Language Disorders*, 34(4), 313–328. https://doi.org/10.1097/TLD.0000000000000037

Dennett, D. C. (1978). Beliefs About Beliefs. *Behavioral and Brain Sciences*, 1(4), 568–570. https://doi.org/10.1017/S0140525X00076664

Devine, R. T., and Hughes, C. (2014). Relations Between False Belief Understanding and Executive Function in Early Childhood: A Meta-Analysis. *Child Development*, 85, 1777–1794. https://doi.org/10.1111/cdev.12237

Doherty, M. (2008). *Theory of Mind*. London: Psychology Press. https://doi.org/10.4324/9780203929902

Doherty, M., and Perner, J. (1998). Metalinguistic Awareness and Theory of mind: Just Two Words for the Same Thing? *Cognitive Development*, 13(3), 279–305. https://doi.org/10.1016/S0885-2014(98)90012-0

Doherty, M., and Perner, J. (2020). Mental Files: Developmental Integration of Dual Naming and Theory of Mind. *Developmental Review*, 56, 100909. https://doi.org/10.1016/j.dr.2020.100909

Dörrenberg, S., Rakoczy, H., and Liszkowski, U. (2018). How (not) to Measure Infant Theory of Mind: Testing the Replicability and Validity of Four Non-verbal Measures. *Cognitive Development*, 46, 12–30. https://doi.org/10.1016/j.cogdev.2018.01.001

Duh, S., Paik, J. H., Miller, P. H., Gluck, S. C., Li, H., and Himelfarb, I. (2016). Theory of Mind and Executive Function in Chinese Preschool Children. *Developmental Psychology*, 52(4), 582–591. https://doi.org/10.1037/a0040068

Dunn, J., and Dale, N. (1984). I a Daddy: 2-Year-Olds' Collaboration in Joint Pretend with Sibling and with Mother. In I. Bretherton (Ed.), *Symbolic Play*, 131–158. New York: Academic Press. https://doi.org/10.1016/B978-0-12-132680-7.50009-0

Elekes, F., Varga, M., and Király, I. (2016). Evidence for Spontaneous Level-2 Perspective Taking in Adults. *Consciousness and Cognition*, 41, 93–103. https://doi.org/10.1016/j.concog.2016.02.010

Feldman Barrett, F., Adolphs, R., Marsella, S., Martinez, A. M., and Pollak, S. D. (2019). Emotional Expressions Reconsidered: Challenges to Inferring Emotion From Human Facial Movements. *Psychological Science in the Public Interest*, 20(1), 1–68. https://doi.org/10.1177/1529100619832930

Fiebich, A. (2015). *Varieties of Social Understanding*. Padaborn: Mentis.

Fiebich, A. (2019). In Defense of Pluralist Theory. *Synthese*. https://doi.org/10.1007/s11229-019-02490-5

Fiebich, A., and Coltheart, M. (2015). Various Ways to Understand Other Minds: Towards a Pluralistic Approach to the Explanation of Social Understanding. *Mind and Language*, 30(3), 235–258. https://doi.org/10.1111/mila.12079

Fiebich, A., Gallagher, S., and Hutto, D. D. (2017). Pluralism, Interaction and the Ontogeny of Social Cognition. In J. Kiverstein (Ed.), *The Routledge Handbook Philosophy of the Social Mind*, 208–221. London: Routledge.

Flavell, J. H. (1988). The Development of Children's Knowledge About the Mind: From Cognitive Connections to Mental Representations. *Developing Theories of Mind*. New York: Cambridge University Press.

Flavell, J. H. (1992). Perspectives on Perspective Taking. *Piaget's Theory: Prospects and Possibilities*. Hillsdale: Lawrence Erlbaum Associates, Inc.

Flavell, J. H., Everett, B. A., Croft, K., and Flavell, E. R. (1981). Young Children's Knowledge About Visual Perception: Further Evidence for the Level 1-Level 2 Distinction. *Developmental Psychology*, 17(1), 99–103. https://doi.org/10.1037/0012-1649.17.1.99

Flavell, J. H., Flavell, E. R., and Green, F. L. (1983). Development of the Appearance-Reality Distinction. *Cognitive Psychology*, 15, 95–120. https://doi.org/10.1177/016502548901200407

Friedman, O., and Leslie, A. M. (2007). The Conceptual Underpinnings of Pretense: Pretending Is not "Behaving-as-if". *Cognition*, 105(1), 103–124. https://doi.org/10.1016/j.cognition.2006.09.007

Gallagher, S. (2001). The Practice of Mind: Theory, Simulation or Primary Interaction? *Journal of Consciousness Studies*, 8(6–7), 83–108.

Gallagher, S., and Hutto, D. D. (2008). Understanding Others through Primary Interaction and Narrative Practice. In J. Zlatev, T. P. Racine, and E. Itkonwn (Eds.), *The Shared Mind: Perspectives on Intersubjectivity*, 17–38. Amsterdam: John Benjamins Publishing Company. https://doi.org/10.1075/celcr.12.04gal

Garnham, W. A., and Ruffman, T. (2001). Doesn't See, Doesn't Know: Is Anticipatory Looking Really Related to Understanding or Belief? *Developmental Science*, 4(1), 94–100. https://doi.org/10.1111/1467-7687.00153

Gennari, S. P., MacDonald, M. C., Postle, B. R., and Seidenberg, M. S. (2007). Context-dependent Interpretation of Words: Evidence for Interactive Neural Processes. *NeuroImage*, 35(3), 1278–1286. https://doi.org/10.1016/J.NEUROIMAGE.2007.01.015

German, T. P., and Leslie, A. M. (2001). Children's Inferences from 'Knowing' to 'Pretending' and 'Believing'. *British Journal of Developmental Psychology*, *19*(1), 59 – 83. https://doi. org/10.1348/026151001165967

Goldman, A. I. (2006). *Simulating Minds*. Oxford: Oxford University Press. https://doi.org/10. 1093/0195138929.001.0001

Gopnik, A. (1993a). How We Know Our Minds: The Illusion of First-person Knowledge of Intentionality. *Behavioral and Brain Sciences*, *16*(01), 1. https://doi.org/10.1017/ S0140525X00028636

Gopnik, A. (1993b). *Mindblindness*. Unpublished Manuscript. Berkeley.

Gopnik, A. (1996). The Scientist as Child. *Philosophy of Science*, *63*(4), 485 – 514. https://doi. org/10.1086/289970

Gopnik, A., and Astington, J. W. (1988). Children's Understanding of Representational Change and Its Relation to the Understanding of False Belief and the Appearance-Reality Distinction. *Child Development*, *59*(1), 26 – 37. https://doi.org/10.2307/1130386

Gopnik, A., and Wellman, H. M. (1992). Why the Child's Theory of Mind Really Is a Theory. *Mind and Language*, *7*(1 – 2), 145 – 171. https://doi.org/10.1111/j.1468-0017.1992.tb00202. x

Gopnik, A., and Wellman, H. M. (2012). Reconstructing Constructivism: Causal Models, Bayesian Learning Mechanisms and the Theory Theory. *Psychological Bulletin*, *138*(6), 1085 – 1108. https://doi.org/10.1037/a0028044.

Gordon, R. M. (1986). Folk Psychology as Simulation. *Mind and Language*, *1*(2), 158 – 171. https://doi.org/10.1111/j.1468-0017.1986.tb00324.x

Grosse Wiesmann, C., Friederici, A. D., Singer, T., and Steinbeis, N. (2017). Implicit and Explicit False Belief Development in Preschool Children. *Developmental Science*, *20*(5), e12445. https://doi.org/10.1111/desc.12445

Haight, W., and Miller, P. J. (1992). The Development of Everyday Pretend Play: A Longitudinal Study of Mothers' Participation. *Merrill-Palmer Quarterly*, *38*(3), 331 – 349.

Hansen, M. B. (2010). If You Know Something, Say Something: Young Children's Problem With False Beliefs. *Frontiers in Psychology*, *1*(July), 1 – 7. https://doi.org/10.3389/fpsyg. 2010.00023

Happé, F. G. E. (1994). An Advanced Test of Theory of Mind: Understanding of Story Characters' Thoughts and Feelings by Able Autistic, Mentally Handicapped, and Normal Children and Adults. *Journal of Autism and Developmental Disorders*, *24*(2), 129 – 154. https://doi.org/10.1007/BF02172093

Hare, B., Call, J., and Tomasello, M. (2001). Do Chimpanzees Know What Conspecifics Know? *Animal Behaviour*, *61*(1), 139 – 151. https://doi.org/10.1006/anbe.2000.1518

Harman, G. (1978). Studying the Chimpanzee's Theory of Mind. *Behavioral and Brain Sciences*, *1*(4), 576 – 577. https://doi.org/10.1017/S0140525X00076743

He, Z., Bolz, M., and Baillargeon, R. (2011). False-belief Understanding in 2.5-year-olds: Evidence from Violation-of-expectation Change-of-location and Unexpected-contents Tasks. *Developmental Science*, *14*(2), 292 – 305. https://doi.org/10.1111/j.1467-7687.2010. 00980.x

He, Z., Bolz, M., and Baillargeon, R. (2012). 2.5-year-olds Succeed at a Verbal Anticipatory-looking False-belief Task. *British Journal of Developmental Psychology*, *30*(1), 14 – 29. https://doi.org/10.1111/j.2044-835X.2011.02070.x

Hedger, J. A., and Fabricius, W. V. (2011). True Belief Belies False Belief: Recent Findings of Competence in Infants and Limitations in 5-Year-Olds, and Implications for Theory of Mind Development. *Review of Philosophy and Psychology, 2*(3), 429–447. https://doi. org/10.1007/s13164-011-0069-9

Helming, K. A., Strickland, B., and Jacob, P. (2016). Solving the Puzzle about Early Belief-Ascription. *Mind and Language, 31*(4), 438–469. https://doi.org/10.1111/mila.12114

Heyes, C. (2014a). False Belief in Infancy: A Fresh Look. *Developmental Science, 17*(5), 647–659. https://doi.org/10.1111/desc.12148

Heyes, C. (2014b). Submentalizing. *Perspectives on Psychological Science, 9*(2), 131–143. https://doi.org/10.1177/1745691613518076

Heyes, C. (2018). *Cognitive Gadgets : The Cultural Evolution of Thinking.* Cambridge, M.A.: The Belknap Press of Harvard University Press.

Hommel, B. (2004). Event Files: Feature Binding in and Across Perception and Action. *Trends in Cognitive Sciences, 8*(11), 494–500. https://doi.org/10.1016/j.tics.2004.08.007

Huemer, M., Perner, J., and Leahy, B. (2018). Mental Files Theory of Mind: When Do Children Consider Agents Acquainted With Different Object Identities? *Cognition, 171*, 122–129. https://doi.org/10.1016/j.cognition.2017.10.011

Hume, D. (1978). *A Treatise of Human Nature.* (L. A. Selby-Bigge and P. H. Nidditch, Eds.) Oxford: Clarendon Press. https://doi.org/10.1093/actrade/9780198245872

Hutto, D. D. (2004). The Limits of Spectatorial Folk Psychology. *Mind and Language, 19*(5), 548–573. https://doi.org/10.1111/j.0268-1064.2004.00272.x

Hutto, D. D. (2008). *Folk Psychological Narratives: The Sociocultural Basis of Understanding Reasons.* Cambridge, M.A.: MIT Press. https://doi.org/10.1080/10848770.2013.791435

Hutto, D. D. (2009). ToM Rules, but It Is not OK. In I. Leudar and A. Costall (Eds.), *Against Theory of Mind*, 221–238. London: Palgrave Macmillan UK. https://doi.org/10.1057/9780230234383_12

Jacob, P. (2020). What Do False-Belief Tests Show? *Review of Philosophy and Psychology, 11*(1), 1–20. https://doi.org/10.1007/s13164-019-00442-z

Jarrold, C., Carruthers, P., Smith, P., and Boucher, J. (1994). Pretend Play: Is It Metarepresentational? *Mind and Language, 9*(4), 445–468. https://doi.org/10.1111/j.1468-0017.1994.tb00318.x

Kahneman, D, Treisman, A., and Gibbs, B. J. (1992). The Reviewing of Object-files: Object Specific Integration of Information. *Cognitive Psychology, 24*, 174–219.

Kahneman, Daniel. (2003). A Perspective on Judgment and Choice. *American Psychologist, 58*(9), 697–720. https://doi.org/10.1037/0003-066X.58.9.697

Kahneman, Daniel. (2011). *Thinking, Fast and Slow.* New York: Farrar, Straus and Giroux.

Kammermeier, M., and Paulus, M. (2018). Do Action-based Tasks Evidence False-Belief Understanding in Young Children? *Cognitive Development, 46*, 31–39. https://doi.org/10.1016/j.cogdev.2017.11.004

Kano, F., Krupenye, C., Hirata, S., and Call, J. (2017). Eye Tracking Uncovered Great Apes' Ability to Anticipate that Other Individuals Will Act According to False Beliefs. *Communicative and Integrative Biology, 10*(2), 1–7. https://doi.org/10.1080/19420889.2017.1299836

Knudsen, B., and Liszkowski, U. (2012). 18-Month-Olds Predict Specific Action Mistakes Through Attribution of False Belief, Not Ignorance, and Intervene Accordingly. *Infancy, 17*(6), 672–691. https://doi.org/10.1111/j.1532-7078.2011.00105.x

Kovács, Á. M., Téglás, E., and Endress, A. D. (2010). The Social Sense: Susceptibility to Others' Beliefs in Human Infants and Adults. *Science*, *330*(6012), 1830–1834. https://doi.org/10.1126/science.1190792

Kulke, L., and Rakoczy, H. (2018). Implicit Theory of Mind – An Overview of Current Replications and Non-replications. *Data in Brief*, *16*, 101–104. https://doi.org/10.1016/j.dib.2017.11.016

Kulke, L., Reiß, M., Krist, H., and Rakoczy, H. (2018). How Robust are Anticipatory Looking Measures of Theory of Mind? Replication Attempts Across the Life Span. *Cognitive Development*, *46*, 97–111. https://doi.org/10.1016/j.cogdev.2017.09.001

Kulke, L., von Duhn, B., Schneider, D., and Rakoczy, H. (2018). Is Implicit Theory of Mind a Real and Robust Phenomenon? Results From a Systematic Replication Study. *Psychological Science*, *29*(6), 888–900. https://doi.org/10.1177/0956797617747090

Leslie, A. M. (1987). Pretense and Representation: The Origins of "Theory of Mind". *Psychological Review*, *94*(4), 412–426. https://doi.org/10.1037/0033-295X.94.4.412

Leslie, A. M. (1988). Some Implications of Pretense for Mechanisms Underlying the Child's Theory of Mind. In *Developing Theories of Mind*, 19–46. New York, NY, US: Cambridge University Press.

Leslie, A. M. (1994). Pretending and Believing: Issues in the Theory of ToMM. *Cognition*, *50*(1–3), 211–238. https://doi.org/10.1016/0010-0277(94)90029-9

Leslie, A. M. (2002). Pretense and Representation Revisited. In N. L. Stein, P. J. Bauer, and M. Rabinowitz (Eds.), *Representation, Memory, and Development: Essays in Honor of Jean Mandler*, 103–115. London: Lawrence Erlbaum Associates.

Leslie, A. M., Friedman, O., and German, T. P. (2004). Core Mechanisms in "Theory of Mind". *Trends in Cognitive Sciences*, *8*(12), 528–533. https://doi.org/10.1016/j.tics.2004.10.001

Leslie, A. M., German, T. P., and Polizzi, P. (2005). Belief-desire Reasoning as a Process of Selection. *Cognitive Psychology*, *50*(1), 45–85. https://doi.org/10.1016/j.cogpsych.2004.06.002

Lewis, D. (1999). Individuation by Acquaintance and by Stipulation. In *Papers in Metaphysics and Epistemology*, Vol. 2, 373–402. Cambridge: Cambridge University Press. https://doi.org/10.1017/CBO9780511625343.023

Lewis, S., Hacquard, V., and Lidz, J. (2012). The Semantics and Pragmatics of Belief Reports in Preschoolers. *Salt 22*, (1), 247–267.

Liao, S. yi, and Szabó Gendler, T. (2011). Pretense and Imagination. *Wiley Interdisciplinary Reviews: Cognitive Science*, *2*(1), 79–94. https://doi.org/10.1002/wcs.91

Lillard, A. (1993). Young Children's Conceptualization of Pretense: Action or Mental Representational State? *Child Development*, *64*(2), 372. https://doi.org/10.2307/1131256

Lillard, A. (1994). Making Sense of Pretence. In C. Lewis and P. Mitchell (Eds.), *Children's Early Understanding of Mind: Origins and Development*, 211–234. Hillsdale: Lawrence Erlbaum Associates.

Lillard, A. (2001). Pretend Play as Twin Earth: A Social-Cognitive Analysis. *Developmental Review*, *21*(4), 495–531. https://doi.org/10.1006/drev.2001.0532

Lillard, A., and Witherington, D. C. (2004). Mothers' Behavior Modifications During Pretense and Their Possible Signal Value for Toddlers. *Developmental Psychology*, *40*(1), 95–113. https://doi.org/10.1037/0012-1649.40.1.95

Liu, D., Wellman, H. M., Tardif, T., and Sabbagh, M. A. (2008). Theory of Mind Development in Chinese Children: A Meta-analysis of False-belief Understanding Across Cultures and

Languages. *Developmental Psychology*, *44*(2), 523–531. https://doi.org/10.1037/0012-1649.44.2.523

Logan, G. D. (1997). Automaticity and Reading: Perspectives from the Instance Theory of Automatization. *Reading & Writing Quarterly*, *13*(2), 123–146. https://doi.org/10.1080/1057356970130203

Low, J. (2010). Preschoolers' Implicit and Explicit False-Belief Understanding: Relations With Complex Syntactical Mastery. *Child Development*, *81*(2), 597–615. https://doi.org/10.1111/j.1467-8624.2009.01418.x

Low, J., Apperly, I. A., Butterfill, S. A., and Rakoczy, H. (2016). Cognitive Architecture of Belief Reasoning in Children and Adults: A Primer on the Two-Systems Account. *Child Development Perspectives*, *10*(3), 184–189. https://doi.org/10.1111/cdep.12183

Mascaro, O., and Morin, O. (2015). Epistemology for Beginners: Two- to Five-Year-Old Children's Representation of Falsity. *PLOS ONE*, *10*(10), e0140658. https://doi.org/10.1371/journal.pone.0140658

Mascaro, O., Morin, O., and Sperber, D. (2017). Optimistic Expectations About Communication Explain Children's Difficulties in Hiding, Lying, and Mistrusting Liars. *Journal of Child Language*, *44*(5), 1041–1064. https://doi.org/10.1017/S0305000916000350

Meristo, M., Falkman, K. W., Hjelmquist, E., Tedoldi, M., Surian, L., and Siegal, M. (2007). Language Access and Theory of Mind Reasoning: Evidence from Deaf Children in Bilingual and Oralist Environments. *Developmental Psychology*, *43*(5), 1156–1169. https://doi.org/10.1037/0012-1649.43.5.1156

Miller, S. A. (2009). Children's Understanding of Second-order Mental States. *Psychological Bulletin*, *135*(5), 749–773. https://doi.org/10.1037/a0016854

Mitchell, P., and Lacohée, H. (1991). Children's Early Understanding of False Belief. *Cognition*, *39*, 107–127.

Moll, H., Khalulyan, A., and Moffett, L. (2017). 2.5-Year-Olds Express Suspense When Others Approach Reality With False Expectations. *Child Development*, *88*(1), 114–122. https://doi.org/10.1111/cdev.12581

Moll, H., Meltzoff, A. N., Merzsch, K., and Tomasello, M. (2013). Taking Versus Confronting Visual Perspectives in Preschool Children. *Developmental Psychology*, *49*(4), 646–654. https://doi.org/10.1037/a0028633

Moll, H., and Tomasello, M. (2012). Three-year-olds Understand Appearance and Reality – Just not About the Same Object at the Same Time. *Developmental Psychology*, *48*(4), 1124–1132. https://doi.org/10.1037/a0025915

Murez, M., and Smortchkova, J. (2014). Singular Thought: Object-files, Person-files, and the Sortal PERSON. *Topics in Cognitive Science*, *6*(4), 632–646. https://doi.org/10.1111/tops.12110

Mutter, B., Alcorn, M. B., and Welsh, M. (2006). Theory of Mind and Executive Function: Working-Memory Capacity and Inhibitory Control as Predictors of False-Belief Task Performance. *Perceptual and Motor Skills*, *102*(3), 819–835. https://doi.org/10.2466/pms.102.3.819-835

Newen, A. (2010). Phenomenal Concepts and Mental Files: Phenomenal Concepts Are Theory-based. *Philosophia Naturalis*, *47–48*(1–2), 155–183. https://doi.org/10.3196/003180211796334183

Newen, A. (2015). Understanding Others – The Person Model Theory. *Open MIND*, *26*, 1–28. https://doi.org/10.15502/9783958570320

Newen, A. (2017). Defending the Liberal-content View of Perceptual Experience: Direct Social Perception of Emotions and Person Impressions. *Synthese, 194*(3), 761–785. https://doi.org/10.1007/s11229-016-1030-3

Newen, A., and Starzak, T. (2020). How to Ascribe Beliefs to Animals. *Mind and Language*, 1–19. https://doi.org/10.1111/mila.12302

Newen, A., and Wolf, J. (2020). The Situational Mental File Account of the False Belief Tasks: A New Solution of the Paradox of False Belief Understanding. *Review of Philosophy and Psychology*, 11, 717–744. https://doi.org/10.1007/s13164-020-00466-w

Nichols, S., and Stich, S. (2000). A Cognitive Theory of Pretense. *Cognition, 74*(2), 115–147. https://doi.org/10.1016/S0010-0277(99)00070-0

Nisbett, R. E., and Wilson, T. D. (1977). Telling More Than We Can Know: Verbal Reports on Mental Processes. *Psychological Review, 84*(3), 231–259. https://doi.org/10.1037/0033-295X.84.3.231

O'Hare, A. E., Bremner, L., Nash, M., Happé, F., and Pettigrew, L. M. (2009). A Clinical Assessment Tool for Advanced Theory of Mind Performance in 5 to 12 Year Olds. *Journal of Autism and Developmental Disorders, 39*(6), 916–928. https://doi.org/10.1007/s10803-009-0699-2

Onishi, K. H., and Baillargeon, R. (2005). Do 15-month-old Infants Understand False Beliefs? *Science, 308*(5719), 255–258. https://doi.org/10.1126/science.1107621

Osterhaus, C., Koerber, S., and Sodian, B. (2016). Scaling of Advanced Theory-of-Mind Tasks. *Child Development, 87*(6), 1971–1991. https://doi.org/10.1111/cdev.12566

Penn, D. C., and Povinelli, D. J. (2007). On the Lack of Evidence That Non-human Animals Possess Anything Remotely Resembling a "Theory of Mind". *Philosophical Transactions of the Royal Society B: Biological Sciences, 362*(1480), 731–744. https://doi.org/10.1098/rstb.2006.2023

Perner, J. (1991). *Understanding the Representational Mind. Understanding the Representational Mind.* Cambridge, M.A.: MIT Press.

Perner, J. (2016). Referential and Cooperative Bias: In Defence of an Implicit Theory of Mind. *Brains Blog.* Retrieved from http://philosophyofbrains.com/2016/10/17/symposium-on helming-%0Astrickland-and-jacob-solving-the-puzzle-about-early-belief-ascription.aspx. (Last visited 10.11.2017.)

Perner, J., Baker, S., and Hutton, D. (1994). Prelief: The Conceptual Origins of Belief and Pretence. In C. Lewis and P. Mitchell (Eds.), *Children's Early Understanding of Mind: Origins and Development*, 261–286). Hillsdale: Lawrence Erlbaum Associates.

Perner, J., and Brandl, J. L. (2005). File Chanage Semantics for Preschoolers: Alternative Naming and Belief Understanding. *Interaction Studies, 6*(3), 483–501.

Perner, J., Huemer, M., and Leahy, B. (2015). Mental Files and Belief: A Cognitive Theory of how Children Represent Belief and Its Intensionality. *Cognition, 145*, 77–88. https://doi.org/10.1016/j.cognition.2015.08.006

Perner, J., and Leahy, B. (2016). Mental Files in Development: Dual Naming, False Belief, Identity and Intensionality. *Review of Philosophy and Psychology, 7*(2), 491–508. https://doi.org/10.1007/s13164-015-0235-6

Perner, J., Leekam, S. R., and Wimmer, H. (1987). Three-year-olds' Difficulty With False Belief: The Case for a Conceptual Deficit. *British Journal of Developmental Psychology, 5*(2), 125–137. https://doi.org/10.1111/j.2044-835X.1987.tb01048.x

Perner, J., Priewasser, B., and Roessler, J. (2018). The Practical Other: Teleology and its Development. *Interdisciplinary Science Reviews*, *43*(2), 99–114. https://doi.org/10.1080/03080188.2018.1453246

Perner, J., Rendl, B., and Garnham, A. (2007). Objects of Desire, Thought, and Reality: Problems of Anchoring Discourse Referents in Development. *Mind and Language*, *22*(5), 475–513. https://doi.org/10.1111/j.1468-0017.2007.00317.x

Perner, J., and Roessler, J. (2010). Causing Human Action: New Perspectives on the Causal Theory of Action. In J. Aguilar and A. Buckareff (Eds.), *Causing Human Action: New Perspectives on the Causal Theory of Action*, 199–228. Cambridge, M.A.: Bradford Book.

Perner, J., and Ruffman, T. (2005). Infants' Insight into the Mind: How Deep? *Science*, *308*(5719), 214–216. https://doi.org/10.1126/science.1111656

Perner, J., Ruffman, T., and Leekam, S. R. (1994). Theory of Mind Is Contagious: You Catch It from Your Sibs. *Child Development*, *65*(4), 1228. https://doi.org/10.2307/1131316

Perner, J., Stummer, S., Sprung, M., and Doherty, M. (2002). Theory of Mind Finds its Piagetian Perspective: Why Alternative Naming Comes With Understanding Belief. *Cognitive Development*, *17*(3–4), 1451–1472. https://doi.org/10.1016/S0885-2014(02)00127-2

Perner, J., and Wimmer, H. (1985). "John Thinks That Mary Thinks That…". Attribution of Second-order Beliefs by 5- to 10-year-old Children. *Journal of Experimental Child Psychology*, *39*(3), 437–471. https://doi.org/10.1016/0022-0965(85)90051-7

Peterson, C. C., Wellman, H. M., and Liu, D. (2005). Steps in Theory-of-Mind Development for Children With Deafness or Autism. *Child Development*, *76*(2), 502–517. https://doi.org/10.1111/j.1467-8624.2005.00859.x

Phillips, J., and Norby, A. (2019). Factive Theory of Mind. *Mind and Language*, 1–24. https://doi.org/10.1111/mila.12267

Piaget, J. (1962). *Play, Dreams, and Imitation in Childhood*. New York: Norton.

Poulin-Dubois, D., Rakoczy, H., Burnside, K., Crivello, C., Dörrenberg, S., Edwards, K., … Ruffman, T. (2018). Do Infants Understand False Beliefs? We Don't Know yet – A Commentary on Baillargeon, Buttelmann and Southgate's Commentary. *Cognitive Development*, *48*, 302–315. https://doi.org/10.1016/J.COGDEV.2018.09.005

Povinelli, D. J., and Vonk, J. (2003). Chimpanzee Minds: Suspiciously Human? *Trends in Cognitive Sciences*, *7*(4), 157–160. https://doi.org/10.1016/S1364-6613(03)00053-6

Premack, D., and Woodruff, G. (1978). Does the Chimpanzee Have a Theory of Mind? *Behavioral and Brain Sciences*, *1*(4), 515–526. https://doi.org/10.1017/S0140525X00076512

Priewasser, B., Rafetseder, E., Gargitter, C., and Perner, J. (2018). Helping as an Early Indicator of a Theory of Mind: Mentalism or Teleology? *Cognitive Development*, *46*, 69–78. https://doi.org/10.1016/j.cogdev.2017.08.002

Psouni, E., Falck, A., Boström, L., Persson, M., Sidén, L., and Wallin, M. (2019). Together I Can! Joint Attention Boosts 3- to 4-Year-Olds' Performance in a Verbal False-Belief Test. *Child Development*, *90*(1), 35–50. https://doi.org/10.1111/cdev.13075

Pyers, J. E., and Senghas, A. (2009). Language Promotes False-belief Understanding: Evidence from Learners of a New Sign Language. *Psychological Science*, *20*(7), 805–812. https://doi.org/10.1111/j.1467-9280.2009.02377.x

Rakoczy, H. (2006). Pretend Play and the Development of Collective Intentionality. *Cognitive Systems Research*, *7*(2–3), 113–127. https://doi.org/10.1016/j.cogsys.2005.11.008

Rakoczy, H. (2007). Play, Games, and the Development of Collective Intentionality. *New Directions for Child and Adolescent Development, 115*, 53 – 67. https://doi.org/10.1002/cd.182

Rakoczy, H. (2008a). Pretence as Individual and Collective Intentionality. *Mind and Language, 23*(5), 499 – 517. https://doi.org/10.1111/j.1468-0017.2008.00357.x

Rakoczy, H. (2008b). Taking Fiction Seriously: Young Children Understand the Normative Structure of Joint Pretence Games. *Developmental Psychology, 44*(4), 1195 – 1201. https://doi.org/10.1037/0012-1649.44.4.1195

Rakoczy, H. (2017). In Defense of a Developmental Dogma: Children Acquire Propositional Attitude Folk Psychology Around Age 4. *Synthese, 194*(3), 689 – 707. https://doi.org/10.1007/s11229-015-0860-8

Rakoczy, H., and Tomasello, M. (2006). Two-year-Olds Grasp the Intentional Structure of Pretense Acts. *Developmental Science, 9*(6), 557 – 564. https://doi.org/10.1111/j.1467-7687.2006.00533.x

Rakoczy, H., Tomasello, M., and Striano, T. (2004). Young Children Know That Trying is not Pretending: A Test of the "Behaving-as-if" Construal of Children's Early Concept of Pretense. *Developmental Psychology, 40*(3), 388 – 399. https://doi.org/10.1037/0012-1649.40.3.388

Rakoczy, H., Tomasello, M., and Striano, T. (2005). On Tools and Toys: How Children Learn to Act on and Pretend With Virgin Objects'. *Developmental Science, 8*(1), 57 – 73. https://doi.org/10.1111/j.1467-7687.2005.00393.x

Rakoczy, Warneken, F., and Tomasello, M. (2007). "This Way!", "No! That Way!" – 3-year-olds Know That Two People Can Have Mutually Incompatible Desires. *Cognitive Development, 22*(1), 47 – 68. https://doi.org/10.1016/j.cogdev.2006.08.002

Recanati, F. (2012). *Mental Files.* Oxford: Oxford University Press. https://doi.org/10.1093/acprof:oso/9780199659982.001.0001

Reddy, V. (2008). *How Infants Know Minds.* Cambridge, M.A.: Harvard University Press.

Reddy, V., and Morris, P. (2004). Participants Don't Need Theories. *Theory and Psychology, 14*(5), 647 – 665. https://doi.org/10.1177/0959354304046177

Repacholi, B. M., and Gopnik, A. (1997). Early Reasoning About Desires: Evidence from 14- and 18-month-olds. *Developmental Psychology, 33*(1), 12 – 21. https://doi.org/10.1037/0012-1649.33.1.12

Riggs, K. J., and Robinson, E. J. (1995). What People Say and What They Think: Children's Judgements of False Belief in Relation to Their Recall of False Messages. *British Journal of Developmental Psychology, 13*(3), 271 – 284. https://doi.org/10.1111/j.2044-835x.1995.tb00679.x

Roby, E., and Scott, R. M. (2016). Rethinking the Relationship Between Social Experience and False-belief Understanding: A Mentalistic Account. *Frontiers in Psychology, 7*, 1 – 7. https://doi.org/10.3389/fpsyg.2016.01721

Rubio-Fernández, P. (2013). Perspective Tracking in Progress: Do not Disturb. *Cognition, 129*(2), 264 – 272. https://doi.org/10.1016/j.cognition.2013.07.005

Rubio-Fernández, P. (2018). What Do Failed (and Successful) Replications with the Duplo Task Show? *Cognitive Development, 48*, 316 – 320. https://doi.org/10.1016/j.cogdev.2018.07.004

Rubio-Fernández, P., and Geurts, B. (2013). How to Pass the False-belief Task Before Your Fourth Birthday. *Psychological Science, 24*(1), 27 – 33. https://doi.org/10.1177/0956797612447819

Ruffman, T., Aitken, J., Wilson, A., Puri, A., and Taumoepeau, M. (2018). A Re-Examination of the Broccoli Task: Implications for Children's Understanding of Subjective Desire. *Cognitive Development, 46*, 79–85. https://doi.org/10.1016/j.cogdev.2017.08.001

Ruffman, T., Perner, J., Naito, M., Parkin, L., and Clements, W. A. (1998). Older (but not Younger) Siblings Facilitate False Belief Understanding. *Developmental Psychology, 34*(1), 161–174. https://doi.org/10.1037/0012-1649.34.1.161

Ruffman, T., Slade, L., and Crowe, E. (2002). The Relation between Children's and Mothers? Mental State Language and Theory-of-Mind Understanding. *Child Development, 73*(3), 734–751. https://doi.org/10.1111/1467-8624.00435

Rupert, R. D. (2009). *Cognitive Systems and the Extended Mind.* New York: Oxford University Press. https://doi.org/10.1093/acprof:oso/9780195379457.001.0001

Samson, D., and Apperly, I. A. (2010). There is More to Mind Reading than Having Theory of Mind Concepts: New Directions in Theory of Mind Research. *Infant and Child Development, 18*(6), 443–454. https://doi.org/10.1002/icd.678

Samson, D., Apperly, I. A., Braithwaite, J. J., Andrews, B. J., and Bodley Scott, S. E. (2010). Seeing it Their Way: Evidence for Rapid and Involuntary Computation of What Other People See. *Journal of Experimental Psychology: Human Perception and Performance, 36*(5), 1255–1266. https://doi.org/10.1037/a0018729

Schneider, D., Nott, Z. E., and Dux, P. E. (2014). Task Instructions and Implicit Theory of Mind. *Cognition, 133*(1), 43–47. https://doi.org/10.1016/j.cognition.2014.05.016

Scholl, B. J., and Leslie, A. M. (2001). Minds, Modules, and Meta-Analysis. *Child Development, 72*(3), 696–701. https://doi.org/10.1111/1467-8624.00308

Schwitzgebel, E. (2008). The Unreliability of Naive Introspection. *Philosophical Review, 117*(2), 245–273. https://doi.org/10.1215/00318108-2007-037

Scott, R. M. (2017). The Developmental Origins of False-Belief Understanding. *Current Directions in Psychological Science, 26*(1), 68–74. https://doi.org/10.1177/0963721416673174

Scott, R. M., and Baillargeon, R. (2009). Which Penguin Is This? Attributing False Beliefs About Object Identity at 18 Months. *Child Development, 80*(4), 1172–1196. https://doi.org/10.1111/j.1467-8624.2009.01324.x

Scott, R. M., and Baillargeon, R. (2017). Early False-Belief Understanding. *Trends in Cognitive Sciences, 21*(4), 237–249. https://doi.org/10.1016/j.tics.2017.01.012

Scott, R. M., He, Z., Baillargeon, R., and Cummins, D. (2012). False-belief Understanding in 2.5-year-olds: Evidence from Two Novel Verbal Spontaneous-response Tasks. *Developmental Science, 15*(2), 181–193. https://doi.org/10.1111/j.1467-7687.2011.01103.x

Siegal, M., and Beattie, K. (1991). Where to Look First for Children's Knowledge of False Beliefs. *Cognition, 38*(1), 1–12. https://doi.org/10.1016/0010-0277(91)90020-5

Slade, A. (1987). A Longitudinal Study of Maternal Involvement and Symbolic Play during the Toddler Period. *Child Development, 58*(2), 367–375. https://doi.org/10.2307/1130513

Sobel, D. M., Capps, L. M., and Gopnik, A. (2005). Ambiguous Figure Perception and Theory of Mind Understanding in Children with Autistic Spectrum Disorders. *British Journal of Developmental Psychology, 23*(2), 159–174. https://doi.org/10.1348/026151004X20694

Sodian, B., Thoermer, C., and Metz, U. (2007). Now I See It but You Don't: 14-month-olds Can Represent Another Person's Visual Perspective. *Developmental Science, 10*(2), 199–204. https://doi.org/10.1111/j.1467-7687.2007.00580.x

Song, H., and Baillargeon, R. (2008). Infants' Reasoning About Others' False Perceptions. *Developmental Psychology*, *44*(6), 1789–1795. https://doi.org/10.1037/a0013774

Southgate, V. (2013). Early Manifestations of Mindreading. In S. Baron-Cohen, H. Tager Flusberg, and M. Lombardo (Eds.), *Understanding Other Minds* (3rd Editio). New York: Oxford University Press. https://doi.org/10.1093/acprof:oso/9780199692972.003.0001

Southgate, V., Chevallier, C., and Csibra, G. (2010). Seventeen-month-olds Appeal to False Beliefs to Interpret Others ' Referential Communication. *Developmental Science*, *13*(6), 907–912. https://doi.org/10.1111/j.1467-7687.2009.00946.x

Southgate, V., Senju, A., and Csibra, G. (2007). Action Anticipation Through Attribution of False Belief by 2-year-olds. *Psychological Science*, *18*(7), 587–592. https://doi.org/10.1111/j.1467-9280.2007.01944.x

Spaulding, S. (2018). *How We Understand Others : Philosophy and Social Cognition*. London: Routledge. https://doi.org/10.4324/9781315396064

Sterelny, K. (2010). Minds: Extended or Scaffolded? *Phenomenology and the Cognitive Sciences*, *9*(4), 465–481. https://doi.org/10.1007/s11097-010-9174-y

Stich, S., and Tarzia, J. (2015). The Pretense Debate. *Cognition*, *143*, 1–12. https://doi.org/10.1016/j.cognition.2015.06.007

Suddendorf, T., and Whiten, A. (2003). Reinterpreting the Mentality of Apes. In J. Fittness and K. Sterelny (Eds.), *From Mating to Mentality: Evaluating Evolutionary Psychology*, 173–196. Hove: Psychology Press.

Surian, L., Caldi, S., and Sperber, D. (2007). Attribution of Beliefs by 13-month-old Infants. *Psychological Science*, *18*(7), 580–586. https://doi.org/10.1111/j.1467-9280.2007.01943.x

Surtees, A., Samson, D., and Apperly, I. (2016). Unintentional Perspective-taking Calculates Whether Something is Seen, But not How It Is Seen. *Cognition*, *148*, 97–105. https://doi.org/10.1016/j.cognition.2015.12.010

Tomasello, M., Call, J., and Hare, B. (2003). Chimpanzees Versus Humans: It's not That Simple. *Trends in Cognitive Sciences*, *7*(6), 239–240. https://doi.org/10.1016/S1364-6613(03)00107-4

Trevarthen, C. (1979). Communication and Cooperation in Early Infancy: A Description of Primary Intersubjectivity. In M. Bullowa (Ed.), *Before Speech: The Beginning of Interpersonal Communication*, 530–571. Cambridge: Cambridge University Press.

Trevarthen, C., and Hubley, P. (1978). Secondary Intersubjectivity: Confidence, Confiding and Acts of Meaning in the First Year. In A. Lock (Ed.), *Action, Gesture, and Symbol : The Emergence of Language*, 183–229. London: Academic Press. Retrieved from http://ci.nii.ac.jp/naid/10021064103/en/

van der Wel, R. P. R. D., Sebanz, N., and Knoblich, G. (2014). Do People Automatically Track Others' Beliefs? Evidence from a Continuous Measure. *Cognition*, *130*(1), 128–133. https://doi.org/10.1016/j.cognition.2013.10.004

Vierkant, T. (2012). Self-knowledge and Knowing Other Minds: The Implicit/Explicit Distinction as a Tool in Understanding Theory of Mind. *British Journal of Developmental Psychology*, *30*(1), 141–155. https://doi.org/10.1111/j.2044-835X.2011.02068.x

Wang, L., and Leslie, A. M. (2016). Is Implicit Theory of Mind the 'Real Deal'? The Own-Belief/True-Belief Default in Adults and Young Preschoolers. *Mind and Language*, *31*(2), 147–176. https://doi.org/10.1111/mila.12099

Warneken, F., and Tomasello, M. (2007). Helping and Cooperation at 14 Months of Age. *Infancy, 11*(3), 271–294. https://doi.org/https://doi.org/10.1111/j.1532-7078.2007. tb00227.x

Wellman, H. M. (1990). *The Child's Theory of Mind.* Cambridge, M.A.: MIT Press.

Wellman, H. M. (2002). Understanding the Psychological World: Developing a Theory of Mind. In U. Goswami (Ed.), *Handbook of Childhood Cognitive Development,* 167–187. Oxford: Blackwell Publishing Inc.

Wellman, H. M. (2014). *Making Minds : How Theory of Mind Develops.* Oxford: Oxford University Press.

Wellman, H. M., and Bartsch, K. (1988). Young Children's Reasoning About Beliefs. *Cognition, 30*(3), 239–277. https://doi.org/10.1016/0010-0277(88)90021-2

Wellman, H. M., Cross, D., and Watson, J. (2001). Meta-Analysis of Theory-of-Mind Development : The Truth About False Belief. *Child Development, 72*(3), 655–684. https:// doi.org/10.1111/1467-8624.00304

Wellman, H. M., and Liu, D. (2004). Scaling of Theory-of-mind Tasks. *Child Development,* 75(2), 523–541. https://doi.org/10.1111/j.1467-8624.2004.00691.x

Westra, E. (2016). Pragmatic Development and the False Belief Task. *Review of Philosophy and Psychology, 8*(2), 235–257. https://doi.org/10.1007/s13164-016-0320-5

Westra, E. (2018). Character and Theory of Mind: An Integrative Approach. *Philosophical Studies, 175*(5), 1217–1241. https://doi.org/10.1007/s11098-017-0908-3

Westra, E. (2020). Review Essay of Spaulding's "How We Understand Others: Philosophy and Social Cognition". *Philosophical Psychology.*

Westra, E., and Carruthers, P. (2017). Pragmatic Development Explains the Theory-of-Mind Scale. *Cognition, 158,* 165–176. https://doi.org/10.1016/j.cognition.2016.10.021

Wimmer, H., and Mayringer, H. (1998). False Belief Understanding in Young Children: Explanations Do not Develop Before Predictions. *International Journal of Behavioral Development, 22*(2), 403–422. https://doi.org/10.1080/016502598384441

Wimmer, H., and Perner, J. (1983). Beliefs About Beliefs: Representation and Constraining Function of Wrong Beliefs in Young Children's Understanding of Deception. *Cognition, 13*(1), 103–128. https://doi.org/10.1016/0010-0277(83)90004-5

Wimmer, M., and Doherty, M. (2011). The Development of Ambiguous Figure Perception. *Monographs of the Society for Research in Child Development, 76,* 1–130. https://doi. org/10.1111/j.1540-5834.2011.00589.x

Wolf, J., Coninx, S. (2021). The Role of Mindreading in a Pluralist Framework of Social Cognition, *Proceedings of the Annual Meeting of the Cognitive Science Society.*

Wolf, J., Coninx, S., and Newen, A. (under review). Rethinking Integration of Epistemic Strategies in Social Understanding: Examining the Central Role of Mindreading in Pluralist Accounts.

Woodward, A. (1998). Infants Selectively Encode the Goal Object of an Actor's Reach. *Cognition, 69*(1), 1–34. https://doi.org/10.1016/S0010-0277(98)00058-4

Wyman, E., Rakoczy, H., and Tomasello, M. (2009). Young Children Understand Multiple Pretend Identities in Their Object Play. *British Journal of Developmental Psychology,* 27(2), 385–404. https://doi.org/10.1348/026151008X322893

Zelazo, P. D. (2006). The Dimensional Change Card Sort (DCCS): A Method of Assessing Executive Function in Children. *Nature Protocols, 1*(1), 297–301. https://doi.org/10.1038/ nprot.2006.46

Subject Index

Author Index

www.ingramcontent.com/pod-product-compliance
Lightning Source LLC
Chambersburg PA
CBHW020200090426
42734CB00008B/893